NEGOTIATE YOUR COMMERCIAL LEASE

NEGOTIATE YOUR COMMERCIAL LEASE

Dale R. Willerton

Self-Counsel Press
(a division of)
International Self-Counsel Press Ltd.
USA   Canada

Self-Counsel Press acknowledges the financial support of the Government of Canada through the Book Publishing Industry Development Program (BPIDP) for our publishing activities.

Printed in Canada.

First edition: 1998; Reprinted: 1999

Second edition: 2003

Canadian Cataloguing in Publication Data

Willerton, Dale R., (Dale Ralph),1962-
    Negotiate your commercial lease / Dale R. Willerton. — 2nd ed.

    (Self-counsel business series)
    ISBN 1-55180-421-2

    1. Commercial lease — Canada. 2. Landlord and tenant — Canada. 3.
Negotiation in business. I. Title. II. Series.
KE695.C6W54 2003   658.15′242   C2002-911548-5
KF593.C6W54 2003

Self-Counsel Press
(a division of)
International Self-Counsel Press Ltd.

1704 N. State Street	1481 Charlotte Road
Bellingham, WA 98225	North Vancouver, BC V7J 1H1
USA	Canada

To Linda, the love of my life.

CONTENTS

NOTICE TO READERS

ACKNOWLEDGEMENTS

Many special people have made a great difference in my life, thank you.

My wife, Linda; Jean Willerton, my mother whom I love dearly; Ralph Willerton, my late father and best supporter; Alana and Jessie, two great daughters; Pam Meurs, a tremendous office manager; and Ken and Ann Dennis, my spiritual mentors.

INTRODUCTION

Dear Tenants,

Read this book once if you are about to negotiate your lease renewal — and read it twice if you intend to negotiate your first commercial lease.

This book contains the nuts and bolts that every business owner needs in order to assemble a favorable lease agreement or renewal. Since tenants unfortunately make many mistakes throughout the leasing process, this is not only a *how-to* book but also a *how-not-to* book.

There are two key factors that must be comprehended if you intend to use this book to its fullest. The first is *knowledge:* your knowledge of what is most negotiable and how to best negotiate for it is critical. The second factor is your personal *negotiating skill.* For example, knowing that a personal guarantee is not in your best interests is a far cry from knowing how to make the personal guarantee go away. This book and the many stories contained within will give you knowledge and insight you can use immediately, and for that reason will, to a large degree, make you a better negotiator.

However, really successful negotiators are persuasive communicators with industry knowledge plus practical real-world experience. Unfortunately, this describes the average commercial leasing broker better than the average tenant. By writing about the lease negotiating process in this book, I have attempted to level the playing field, all things considered.

Keep an open mind while you read, since there are exceptions to many of the guidelines I give. You should not expect to successfully negotiate everything in this book — that would be unrealistic. Nevertheless, you are the customer. If you can create competition for your tenancy rather than hand your tenancy to the landlord on a silver platter you will be starting down the right path. After all, how badly a landlord wants your tenancy will partially dictate how good of a deal you can ultimately negotiate.

Be sure to e-mail me your story, situation or leasing questions to <DaleWillerton@TheLeaseCoach.com>. Every inquiry will be answered.

Dale R. Willerton
The Lease Coach®
Certified Lease Consultant

 Remember: In leasing, tenants don't get what they deserve, they get what they negotiate!

CHAPTER 1
THE COMMERCIAL LEASE AGREEMENT

It's true: lease agreements are boring. This is why so many tenants don't read them. Therefore it is with much reservation that I put this section at the beginning of my book. If you can't get through the first few pages, how will you get to the good stuff right? Consider this your permission to skip around the chapters and come back to this one later. You will benefit equally from this book whether you read it back to front or front to back.

1. What Is a Commercial Lease Agreement?

You likely already know that a commercial lease agreement is a binding contract between two parties: the tenant and the landlord. The agreement can be verbal on deals with a term of one year or less (although I don't recommend this; see the discussion of written contracts in section **3.** below). Usually, for a lease agreement to be binding on a term longer than a year, it must be in writing. However, all commercial real estate laws are set and governed by either the state or province.

 For your own protection, make sure all your lease terms are in writing.

Lease agreements are often preceded by an offer to lease. The offer to lease is often only a few pages in length, and is considered a binding document covering the basic business terms, such as rental rate, length of term and commencement date. The offer to lease is a matter of convenience for both you and the landlord. If you can't agree to the points on the offer, there is no point spending time on the longer, formal lease agreement. In most cases, the lease agreement, once executed, will supersede the offer to lease. Many of the negotiating points discussed in this book are ones that should be made at the offer to lease stage.

Formal lease agreements can and do vary in length, more often than not running between 35 to 60 pages. A short lease agreement favors the tenant simply by excluding many clauses and conditions which could potentially favor the landlord, whereas a 60-page lease agreement will leave nothing to the imagination. Every possible scenario or situation will be included, accompanied by the consequences, mostly to the tenant. Only a small part of the lease agreement represents the actual working business terms. At least 80 percent of the agreement defines wording, clarifies terms, and overall serves to protect the landlord's rights while outlining particular remedies. Since, courts will look at the intent of the parties who enter into a lease agreement, the landlord will use long sentences and legalese to define words and explain conditions in an attempt to leave no room for misinterpretation of the document's intent, regardless of what you might think it says. Frequently, tenants misinterpret words and phrases or fail to make certain the terms and conditions of the offer to lease were in fact included in the formal lease agreement. When I review lease documents for tenants, approximately 20 percent of the time the landlord's administrative staff make mistakes in preparing the formal lease agreement. From getting the tenant's name incorrect to miscalculating rental rates and leaving out the free rent, you really can't be too careful. Tenants who used to turn to lawyers for lease document reviews are now coming to lease consultants who can provide more user-friendly advice, often for a much more reasonable fee.

If there is mutual mistake, the party that drew up the offer to lease or lease agreement is usually found at fault. In one case of mutual mistake, a tenant's rent per square foot was inaccurately multiplied by the area stated on the lease agreement: the tenant was paying more rent than actually required. In another instance, the lease term was to be five years, but because of a simple error in dates, the term was stated in the agreement as six years. In both these cases, as in other mutual mistake instances, unless the landlord is prepared to make the necessary adjustments to the agreement, the tenant has grounds to have the lease agreement voided based on the legal principle of mutual mistake.

Most tenants view the commercial lease agreement as a necessary evil. However, don't forget that some developer has invested millions of dollars to construct a building that will provide a home for your business. If you can't agree on the formal lease agreement, the sheer number of properties from which you can choose to lease space puts the smart tenant in the driver's seat

2. Essential Elements of a Commercial Lease Agreement

A lease agreement must include certain elements to be lawfully binding, or else it could be deemed voidable. These nine essential elements are —

(a) the parties to the agreement;

(b) the location of the premises, stated with certainty;

(c) the area of the premises and measurement standard;

(d) the term (or length) of the lease and the commencement date;

(e) the amount of rent to be paid, and when and where payment is to be made;

(f) the operating cost, and when payment is due;

(g) the fixturing period or possession date;

(h) the date of agreement and authorized signatories; and

(i) some form of consideration to consummate the deal.

A consideration clause is usually something like, "In consideration for the sum of ten dollars, paid and received, the tenant and landlord agree as follows...." A court will never judge on whether the consideration paid was just and fair, only whether a legal agreement or contract was made because money changed hands as part of the transaction.

Other points usually covered in the agreement are the personal guarantees, if any; conditions of termination and/or relocation; default remedies; renewal option; and inducements or allowances.

3. Make Sure It's in Writing

Verbal agreements and the intent of the parties in such agreements are admissible in court and are being considered more and more by judges. However, verbal agreements are more open to misunderstandings between the parties than are written agreements. If it's important enough to talk about, include it in the written offer to lease as well as in the formal lease agreement. Property managers and leasing brokers come and go, are transferred or fired. You are always safer assuming nothing and making sure all terms and conditions are in writing: the person you trust to honor your verbal agreement may not be around (or even remember the conversation) when you need them.

Tenants often make false assumptions based on points the realtor has implied but which are not written into the agreement. For example, month-to-month tenants may wrongly assume that they will have first right to lease their space on a longer term basis but if this is not in the agreement, the leasing broker has the right to make a better deal with another party and give the monthly tenant 30 days' notice to vacate.

It is important to include in the agreement any verbal claims the leasing broker or landlord makes. Also include any written claim the leasing broker or landlord makes or shows you as encouragement to lease. Let's say that you were persuaded to lease a space by the broker's claim that 65,000 vehicles per day drive by that property. Later, you read a city survey stating that the traffic count is only 30,000 vehicles per day. You will want the broker's claim to be in writing to be sure you have reasonable recourse in such situations.

The same advice applies to negotiating lease renewals. When a client and I met with his landlord, a number of renewal points were discussed and agreed upon. I knew it would be months before the landlord drafted the documents, so I sent a confirmation letter the following day outlining what had been agreed upon at the meeting. A few months later the landlord's representatives drafted a document that did not correspond with the points agreed to in the meeting. By producing the letter I had written immediately following the meeting, I saved my clients thousands of dollars because the landlord could not dispute the facts. Sending this type of follow-up letter is not binding on the other party but certainly is evidentiary.

Don't be misled by site plans:

If the offer to lease includes a site plan showing who the neighboring tenants are, be sure to verify them. Some leasing brokers or landlords offer site plans showing tenants with whom they are still negotiating, and some site plans show tenants who appear to be in business but may be moving soon when their leases expire. Confirm who your neighbors are.

Most lease agreements contain a clause for the landlord's protection which states that the agreement constitutes "the entire agreement." A shopping center I once managed for an absentee landlord always had disgruntled tenants who claimed the local leasing brokers had made verbal representations to them. I would sympathize with them, but had to refer them to the clause in their lease agreements that said, "this is the entire agreement." Even if you have a letter from the broker or landlord supporting your claim, unless the claim is incorporated into the actual lease agreement, there is a high probability it is not enforceable.

Often, tenants are caught by what the lease agreement does not say rather than what it does say. For example, relocation clauses are standard. When a landlord sent me the formal lease agreement for my client, it contained a relocation clause. However, what the lease agreement neglected to state was who would pay for the relocation. It should have said the landlord would pay all relocation expenses, which is what I negotiated into the agreement. When tenants read leases, they only look at what it says. When I review a lease document for a client, I'm looking for what is left out that should be included.

A tenant came to me once because she wanted to close her business and assign the lease agreement to another tenant. She found someone to take over her lease but the landlord would not agree to the change in use for the premises. The tenant was operating a bottled water company but the new proposed use was for a dog grooming salon. The tenant assumed she could assign the lease to anyone she wanted but that was not what the fine print in the lease agreement said.

Examples of other common disputes in leases include a tenant putting up temporary pullaway roadside signage; and parking allocation disagreements (for example, if one tenant's customers always park in front of another tenant's store). Hours of operation, property upkeep by the landlord, and misunderstood renewal options are also often problematic. Try to think if any situations could become issues for you, and make sure they are covered in the lease agreement. Take nothing for granted; making assumptions can only lead to disappointment.

CHAPTER 2
SELECTING THE BEST SITE FOR YOUR BUSINESS

When I do site selection for a tenant, I am not looking for the cheapest location I can find, but rather the location that will enable the tenant to maximize his or her sales revenues. It's one thing to pay too much rent for a location, but when you pick the wrong location you're sunk. Let me explain with a story about a business owner who wanted to open a restaurant. He attended my leasing seminar and hired me to consult and coach him. The location he picked was terrible and I told him so. Unfortunately he did not take my advice and invested almost $100,000 in getting started. Within two months he couldn't pay the rent and closed out, losing an $8,000 deposit and more. All of this could have been avoided if a proper location had been selected in the first place.

If your lease is coming up for renewal and your business is under-performing, perhaps you need to consider a relocation.

The problem with many businesses is that they under-perform, not that they go broke. If your business is doing $550,000 in sales but it could be doing $750,000 or more in a better location, then what are you waiting for? Look into moving. A great business opportunity in a poor location will soon become a poor business.

1. Consider All the Factors

You can't invest too much time searching for the right location for your business. The challenge of selecting the best location for your business is often twofold. First you must determine what is the right type of location for your particular business use, as well as where you can find such a location. Second, you need to determine what you can afford to pay for such a space.

When determining the right location, consider factors such as a good tenant mix, proper storefront exposure, accessibility to drive-by or walk-by traffic, available parking, local competition, signage, building image, and security.

 It is better to have negotiated a poor lease agreement on the right location than a great deal on the wrong location.

Examine your business's needs. No two businesses will need exactly the same things, in the same priority. This is true for location too. While location is important to all tenants, it's important to different degrees. For example, a cash-and-carry florist needs to be easily accessible to customers. A floral designer specializing in weddings may be able to do good business in a less accessible location since many customers hear of the designer through personal referrals or advertising.

Next you must determine what you can afford to pay for the space so that your business is still profitable. Generally, retail tenants can budget rent between 10 percent and 15 percent of gross sales for gross rent (rent which includes operating costs, discussed in more detail in chapter **8**). This is a guideline only. There is no general guideline for office and warehouse tenants, since business uses vary. Some office tenants pay only 2 percent of gross sales to rent. Others pay a lot more.

Naturally, we are all hoping to secure an equitable agreement that represents good value for our rental dollar. But securing the right location requires that you factor into the equation more than just the rental rate and operating costs. For instance, the most significant location factor for a shopping center tenant is not necessarily even in which mall he or she is located, but where in the shopping center itself the tenant is located. Strip mall tenants must also carefully consider their location, for the same reason. The single most important factor in opening a retail business is site selection. Take your time, and do your homework.

If a retail tenant has to choose between a premium location at what might be too high a rental rate and a less visible or less adequate unit at a lower rate, that tenant will in the long run likely be better off with a superior location despite the higher rental rate. Most retailers who relocate instead of renewing their lease are moving to a better or more costly location. Tenants wishing to relocate within the same building are only occasionally successful with their negotiations and often have to pay all associated costs. So once you've found the right building, invest even more time securing the best possible premises within that building. This also applies to office or even industrial tenants who require a certain corporate image.

However, for many industrial and office-building tenants, location is less important than other factors.

Regardless of what type of business you operate, you must consider customer access to parking, storefront accessibility, building amenities, and the overall tenant mix. Since no two buildings are exactly alike, it is important that they measure up based on more than rental rates. Parking and signage are two other important factors to consider when comparing one building to another, and are discussed in further detail in chapter **12.**

If you are making the transition from home-based to commercial space, you may wish to consider a business or office center. These centers are usually affordable and provide all the professional amenities you will need.

As a consultant, I have experimented with operating out of both a downtown office and a home-based office, and have found that my professional services are more respected and credible when offered from a professional first class downtown office tower. The extra revenue I generate easily offsets the expense of rental space.

2. Allow Enough Time

One day, I received a call from a woman who wanted me to help her get a decent lease renewal. I inquired when her lease was coming up for renewal. She responded with one word: "Tomorrow!" After she attended my seminar, I gave her a few hours of consulting and coaching, and a few weeks later she called to thank me and to say that her new location was cheaper, brighter, cleaner and only a few blocks away from her last location. However, most tenants who leave their lease renewal until the last minute do not have such happy experiences.

New entrepreneurs about to open their first location typically do not allow enough time. If you are a first-time tenant, you should start your site selection process at least 6 months before you plan to open your business. If you are already a tenant, your lease renewal negotiations should be initiated between 9 and 12 months before the lease expires. After all, if you can't get a decent renewal, you will want time to negotiate a new lease and relocate without the pressures that every tenant feels at that time.

One tenant who retained me for consulting told me that he was planning to go into the clothing business. He seemed to be making very detailed plans; I was sure he knew exactly what he was doing. Because of the seasonal nature of his business, a spring opening was critical. Midway through our negotiations with a potential landlord, his stock began to arrive and pile up in his garage. As a result of time pressures, he was forced to settle for a less than desirable location at higher lease rates than necessary because he had already committed himself to this venture before determining from where he would operate the business.

If location and lease terms are important to you (and they should be), don't obligate yourself through a franchise agreement or by buying fixtures or inventory until you have selected a proper location and negotiated the lease agreement. Even the best business concept or franchise will succeed only with a combination of the right location and reasonable rental terms.

In contrast, another seminar attendee, a dentist, spent 18 months researching locations. Wisely, he did not abandon his association with another dentist. He found an excellent location for his practice, we put the lease to bed, and then he cut his ties to his employer. Knowing that he did not have to leave his current position allowed us to negotiate for him from a position of strength. He could have continued working with his employer indefinitely until he found the right location and made the best lease deal.

Giving yourself enough time not only for site selection but also for build-out of the premises (extensive renovations such as changing lighting or the ceiling; adding a heating, ventilation, and air-conditioning (HVAC) unit; or even pouring a cement floor) can be the difference between anguish and exhilaration. It will also eliminate unnecessary stress that is more often than not self-imposed through impractical planning and scheduling.

3. Dealing with Brokers And Leasing Representatives

There are many types of brokers, and leasing representatives. In-house leasing representatives are hired on salary and/or commission to lease the properties of a specific landlord. These in-house leasing representatives are often not licensed brokers and therefore not necessarily governed by the same laws as commercial real estate brokers, who belong to a regional real estate association.

Some brokers generalize: one day they are selling a residential house, the next they are leasing commercial space, and the next they are selling an apartment building. Many commercial brokers/realtors both lease and sell commercial property. Some brokers specialize in leasing downtown office space only, or industrial space only, or retail space only. For simplicity, I will refer from now on to both brokers and realtors as leasing brokers.

It can be valuable for you to talk with leasing brokers before signing a lease or renewal, as they often have valuable "insider" information. However, much of what they say may be opinion only, so you need to keep your guard up at all times and question everything for validity. Remember the old adage of buyer beware when selecting a location for your business through a commercial broker.

Have you ever gone to a job interview just for the practice, just to improve your interview and question-asking skills? If you allow yourself time to view numerous properties, you will be exposed to all types of leasing brokers. You will learn through trial and error what to say and when to resist volunteering information about your situation. Remember, the leasing broker is ethically and legally required to represent the party (i.e., the landlord) who is paying them.

Once you have shortlisted the properties you wish to see, begin viewing them with the listing broker. Do not let one broker show you another broker's listing since this can create commission splitting and dilute your value as a tenant to the brokers. Begin with the least likely property first, working your way up to the most desirable property. The skill and knowledge you gain going through this exercise will undoubtedly serve you well when you reach the best properties you have saved until last. If you view the best location first, you will be tempted to stop there and settle on a deal without having done your site selection homework.

Most leasing brokers earn their living through commission, typically 5 percent to 6 percent of the base or minimum rent for the term of the lease (although a variety of calculations and formulas can be used to determine the commission). Suppose you lease 3,000 square feet at $12 per square foot for a five-year term. The total base or minimum rent will be $36,000 per year, or $180,000 over the five-year term of the lease. If the broker's commission is 5 percent, he or she will earn $9,000 on this deal.

One of my clients was surprised to learn that for space she was considering leasing, the broker's commission was $42,000. When the stakes are high, you had better do your homework, for your own protection. If the broker is a licensed real estate broker (not an in-house employee), you are entitled to know even before negotiations begin what commission he or she is receiving, according to real estate laws. Since laws are governed by state or province, check with your local authorities, then ask the broker directly.

After you get details on the sites you are looking at from each listing broker, be sure to verify the square footage of the premises in which you are interested. Verify that a key tenant, such as a large department store or supermarket, is not about to move out. Ask about any nearby developments under construction: has your competitor already leased space there? Verify that the building you are looking at will not be undergoing major capital improvements that will increase your operating costs — this can be costly to your business. Ask about previous tenants who might have been in the same business as you. If you plan to open a flower shop but are unaware that two previous florists failed in the same building, having this information is certainly valuable. If you don't ask, you may not be told. You must ask the right questions.

Tenants in a small strip mall near my home were recently caught off guard when a Safeway grocery store moved out of the property. None of the business owners who had recently renewed their lease thought to ask if Safeway was staying. While Safeway continues to pay its rent on the vacant space, the landlord cannot put another grocery store into the 25,000 square foot anchor spot, since Safeway has a non competition clause in the lease agreement. So the landlord continues to receive the rent payments from Safeway, but traffic to the strip mall has dropped by 50 percent and the remaining tenants suffer the consequences. Brokers and in-house leasing representatives are required to know this type of information and to answer your questions — if you ask them.

The most common mistake you can make is letting a single leasing broker assist you with viewing a variety of properties. Let me repeat this statement since so many tenants don't understand it: Don't let one broker show you space all over town. Yes, talk to a leasing broker and ask questions. Look at the building the leasing broker's company has listed. But do not let that leasing broker introduce you to another building that is not listed by his or her company. In other words, let the leasing broker know you are willing to look only at buildings for which he or she has active listings to lease. Speak directly to the listing broker for each building in which you are interested. This will result in your obtaining more accurate information more quickly and will avoid commission splitting (where two brokers share the commission), which often results in an inflated rental rate. Approximately 95 percent of all commercial real estate is listed or represented by a particular broker; the broker's contact numbers will be listed on the For Lease sign posted at the building. Remember, if you let a broker go out looking for a location for your business they are really going out looking for a paycheck for themselves. Since not every landlord pays a commission, and because some landlords pay higher commission plus inducements to the broker you may not be getting the service you expect.

In some cases the broker will present you with an offer to lease that states the broker is working in a dual agency capacity. You must cross this off the offer and make your desires known to the broker. It is absolutely critical for you to realize that commercial brokers work for the landlord. They are paid by the landlord to get the best deal for the landlord. So often tenants will refer to someone as their broker; I challenge this since no one can serve two masters.

CHAPTER 3
DETERMINING SQUARE FOOTAGE

As I make the revisions for this book I am negotiating the lease for a tea house. The single most significant contribution I have made to the future of this tenant's business was to counsel them to lease less area than they originally intended to. The tenant had planned to lease 2,400 square feet, but by reducing that to just 1,200 square feet the overhead would be reduced but the tenant could still lease a prime location. For another client, an office tenant, I recommended the opposite approach. The office tenant would be signing a five year lease agreement and planned to add staff along the way. The tenant was so focused on paying as little as possible now that he could not see the future. By leasing a unit with extra space now he could ensure that his company had room to grow into. It would be short-term pain for long-term gain. However, since we implemented some of the strategies below it worked out very much in the tenant's long-term favor in more ways than one.

Why is the area of your premises so important? Most tenants pay their rent by the square foot. If you lease too little space, it might be difficult to run your business. On the other hand, if you lease too many square feet, you'll be wasting rent money. Approximately 30 percent of all commercial space is incorrectly measured. Phantom space, as it is often referred to, is so prevalent in leased space that some companies dedicate themselves to just measuring tenants' premises and ensuring measurements are accurate. The problem of phantom space is discussed in detail in section **4.** below. First, let's look at the optimum size for your premises.

1. Analyze Your Space Requirements

Very few tenants make a clear distinction between monthly gross rent and the rent to be paid per square foot. When a pharmacy owner complained to me that his rent was too high, I surveyed other tenants in the building. The property manager verified what I had suspected: the pharmacist was paying less per square foot than every other tenant in the building. His problem was not in paying too much per square foot but in leasing too much space. We determined that of his 8,000-square-foot store, he really needed only 5,000 square feet. We negotiated to surrender 3,000 square feet to the landlord. This cut the pharmacy's overhead by $45,000 per year and therefore made it a profitable business.

Be sure you are not leasing more space than you really need. Carefully analyze your requirements before signing a lease. Doing so can drastically reduce your costs in rent.

One reason so many tenants find themselves leasing too many square feet is that, as mentioned in the previous chapter, commercial real estate brokers are paid a commission based on area calculations. Very seldom will you hear brokers advising tenants that they don't need all the space. The second reason has to do with what is available in the marketplace. If you need about 2,000 square feet in a strip mall but the only units available are either 2,400 square feet or 2,700 square feet, you are faced with a dilemma.

There are several ways you can solve this problem. First, simply negotiate for a lesser rent per square foot. You will occupy more space than you need but still maintain your ideal monthly gross rent. A second option is to request that a portion of the space be demised off. Recently, I had success with this same issue in a major shopping center. The unit was 1,650 square feet, and the landlord agreed to cut 450 square feet off the back so the tenant could lease and occupy the front 1,200 square feet.

Yet another option to negotiate for reduced area is a graduated arrangement. Let's say that you want a 1,000 square foot space, but the ideal location is 1,435 square feet. When negotiating the rent per square foot, calculate it for the first year at just 1,000 square feet. The second year you might pay rent on 1,100 square feet, the third year on 1,200 square feet, and so on over the five-year term. An arrangement such as this effectively allows you to grow into a larger space over time, while not paying for it all upfront. Starting the rent artificially low and stepping it up over the term has similar results, as long as you can pay the extra rent in the subsequent years.

Whatever you do, don't just settle for whatever size of space the landlord has available. Explain to the leasing broker that it is not really the size of the premises that bothers you but the gross cost of leasing a space that is bigger than you immediately require. While a broker may want you to lease a large commercial retail unit (CRU), the landlord will have a longer, more permanent view of your tenancy, and want you to only bite off what you can chew. Many perfectly good businesses close each year because the tenant has leased more area than they truly need or than they can comfortably pay rent on.

Chapter **7** on negotiating rental rates also discusses a simple strategy to use to get a better deal on your rental rate once you have determined the area of space you need.

2. By What Measurement Standard Is the Space Measured?

Before you can ensure that your space is properly measured, you need to determine what measurement standard the landlord is using to measure it. Every lease agreement should define how the measurement is to be done. In an agreement to lease office space, it might be as simple as stating that the Building Owners and Managers Association (BOMA) standard be used. The lease may or may not go on to define the BOMA standard. For about $30 or $40 you can purchase a copy of this guide from your local BOMA office, located in most major cities.

For most retail and industrial space leases, the agreement will provide a step-by-step guide instructing that measurements be taken from the middle of demising walls to the face of the plate glass windows, and so on. It is important to know that landlords may invent any measurement standards they wish. Scrutinize the lease definition to ensure that they have not changed the standards verbally conveyed by the landlord or leasing broker between viewing the premises and the writing of the agreement.

Once you have determined the standard of measurement, you can measure the premises yourself or hire a professional surveyor to measure it for you. Most companies charge about 10¢ per square foot to measure commercial space. You can usually negotiate a flat rate on larger premises, depending on the degree of difficulty posed by interior partition walls. There is usually an additional charge for the surveyor to draw a detailed floor plan.

3. Rentable versus Usable Space and Gross-Ups

Rental office space often has columns running through it that hold up the building. The space taken up by the columns is considered rentable, but in all practical terms it is not usable. If you take into consideration the hallways and washrooms on any particular office floor, there may be as much as 10 percent of the floor dedicated to common area. So, if you have 3,000 square feet of rentable area, this space will be grossed up by 10 percent and you will pay for 3,300 square feet of space. An actual measurement of the premises, deducting columns and other unusable (but rentable) space, would likely reveal that you have only 2,952 square feet of usable area. Some leases very specifically note these figures, but most do not.

You should have the broker or leasing representative take a few minutes to calculate the actual area of any space you are considering leasing. It is very possible to negotiate a lower gross up on your space. However, the primary reason to go through this exercise is to establish what the gross-up amount really is. If the lease says you will have to pay a gross-up, but does not state what the gross-up amount is, it is like signing for a loan without knowing the interest rate.

4. Phantom Space

Phantom space is the extra area that exists when the leased premises are measured incorrectly. Sometimes, landlords try to cheat tenants by misrepresenting either the size of the premises, the size of the building, or the common areas. One of the easiest ways for a landlord to make an extra 5 percent or 10 percent return on a building is to exaggerate or misrepresent the measurements of the space.

Often, the space is simply measured incorrectly. One measurement I did for a regional chain store showed that the landlord's architect had mismeasured the tenant's space by about 5 percent, or 40 square feet. Since the tenant was paying a premium rent in a downtown shopping center, this mistake resulted in the tenant overpaying $20,000 in rent over seven years. We corrected the measurement, and the tenant was reimbursed for the overpayment. This is an example of a negligent mistake rather than a fraudulent one. Nonetheless it was quite a surprise to the tenant.

Frequently, a landlord will demise a fairly large space, for example, 3,600 square feet, into two smaller units. The landlord will legitimately instruct contractors to put up a wall creating two units, one measuring 1,600 square feet, the other measuring 2,000 square feet. However, if the wall is built even just slightly off to one side, or crookedly, there will be an error in measurement if the space is not accurately measured following the construction.

Often landlords are not even aware of such discrepancies; the figures they are using may have been the measurements represented to them during the purchase of the building. Nonetheless, if discrepancies are proven adjustments should be made to the correct situation.

Sometimes, the discrepancies are in the tenants' favor — tenants may actually have more area than their lease agreement states. As mentioned earlier in this chapter, approximately 30 percent of all commercial space is incorrectly measured. Of this 30 percent, about 20 percent of the errors favor the landlord, 10 percent the tenant.

5. Verifying the Area of Your Premises

Measuring your own space is a lot like hanging wallpaper. It's easier than it looks, but success is achieved with differing degrees of accuracy. However, I recommend that you hire a professional surveyor to do the measurement to ensure accuracy. Look in your yellow pages under surveyors or architects.

If you do decide to measure your space yourself, be sure to look first at the measurement standard clause in your lease agreement. It should tell you clearly how the measurement is calculated.

If, after measuring your space, you find that it is mismeasured in your favor, don't worry, the landlord should not be able to change the lease agreement in terms of base rent to correct the measurement, since the error was his or hers to begin with. Most leases, however, do have a clause that allows the landlord to change or recalculate the operating cost square footage.

If, on the other hand, you have too few square feet, meaning that the mismeasurement is in your landlord's favor, bring it to his or her attention. The landlord will usually verify your measurement and then make the adjustment to the lease. In fact, the landlord is almost always obliged to correct the discrepancy and refund overcharges (although he or she is usually not required to pay you interest on your overpayments). If the landlord refuses to adjust the incorrect measurements or compensate you for overpayments, you have the option of taking the case to court. If you do, you will likely win: legal precedents have been set in these matters.

However, bear in mind that the percentage of the discrepancy in measurement is relevant. One small cafe I had measured for my client was short of the stated lease space by about 100 square feet. Since this represented a 10 percent discrepancy in the cafe's entire area, the landlord could not claim that the higher original measurement was close or even approximate to the actual measurement. However, an error of 120 square feet on a 12,000 square foot area — a discrepancy of only one percent — may be considered acceptable.

 Protect yourself from phantom space by inserting a clause in the lease agreement that forces the landlord to accurately measure the space and make adjustments to the lease accordingly.

To avoid all this, protect yourself at the offer to lease stage. Most offers to lease are on space where the area of the premises has not been certified. If you measure the premises yourself, any discrepancy you discover may be discounted by the landlord as invalid. It's therefore a good idea to add words like the following to the clause in the agreement dealing with square footage: "The landlord will have the area of the premises certified, adjusting the actual square footage accordingly, but not to exceed _____ square feet." In the blank space, put the square footage the landlord has represented the space to be. Most lease agreements state that the landlord has to have a certified architect ascertain the measurement, although a surveyor or engineer trained to do these measurements can also be hired.

If, from the ensuing measurement (made by an expert), you find that the space is smaller than estimated, the landlord must make the appropriate adjustments. If the space is found to be larger than represented to you, the landlord should not be able to raise the measurement in the agreement or the rental rate.

Over the years, I have questioned many tenants whether they have ever verified the square footage of their premises. Only about 10 percent had ever taken the time to do so. Many of you willing to go through this exercise will be pleasantly surprised with the results.

CHAPTER 4
SELECTING THE BEST LEASE TERM (LENGTH)

The term, or length, of your commercial lease is an important part of lease negotiations. However, most tenants do not take enough time to consider that one day they will eventually close down, sell out, expand, downsize, or relocate, and so do not give the term of the lease the consideration it deserves.

The industry-standard lease term is five years. This term, however, is driven more by leasing brokers than landlords, since the longer the term, the greater the broker's commission. Three-year leases are becoming more common, but if you expect to have any kind of significant inducement or tenant allowance, it will be easier to amortize the costs over a longer term, such as five or even seven years. To arrive at a term that works for you, you must analyze your situation.

1. Determining the Best Lease Term for You

One of the first things to consider when determining how many years or months would be the best lease term for you, is when your peak business season is. For example, if you are a shopping center retailer and are beginning your lease October 1, the automatic renewal for that lease, if based on any variation of a 12-month term (i.e., one year, two years, three years, etc.) will come up on September 30 — just before your peak season. Instead of signing a five-year term, consider negotiating a 63-month (5¼ -year) lease term, thereby ensuring one more Christmas season at those premises. Or opt instead for a 54-month (4½-year) lease term to ensure that you will be negotiating from a position of strength at renewal time. After all, it is better to pull out of that location after your peak season than before. For seasonal businesses your lease term should begin going into your peak season and end going into your slow season

 When determining the length of lease best suited to your business, don't fall into the five-year trap. The best month to commence a lease agreement may not be the best month to end a lease term.

For a dance studio I consulted for, we negotiated its new lease term for ten years less two months beginning in September. Dance classes started in the fall and finished at the end of spring. Therefore, if the studio was going to relocate at the end of the term, the tenant would not have to pay rent for July and August, when the dance studio was closed anyway.

Suppose you are opening your accounting and tax preparation office in January. Ask yourself, do I want my lease coming up for renewal right before tax season? And what if this turns out to be a poor location — do I want to be moving desks and filing cabinets in the middle of winter? Relocating and moving your business in the summer is much easier than when there may be snow on the ground. The point here is that you should not be thinking in terms of a five-year lease or even a three-year lease, but rather, how many months you wish to lease for.

Another factor to consider in terms of timing your lease to work for you is the type of business that might move into the space you are leasing after you move out. Prior to becoming a lease consultant, when I was working and leasing space for landlords, I would always try to capitalize on any residual goodwill. When a day-care, confectionery, or cafe moved out of a location, I would always immediately market the space to the same type of user. However, now that I exclusively work for tenants I warn business owners of this tactic. Today, as a lease consultant, when a client of mine is relocating, I sometimes try to arrange the move for several months before the expiration of the lease term to avoid just this scenario. For one such tenant and client I knew the landlord would move in a competitor when the tenant moved to the new location I found. By leaving the space vacant for a few months, the owner was able to redirect all past and future customers to his new location.

2. Month-to-Month Leases

For years I leased my office space on a month-to-month basis, as it meant flexibility for my business. I was never really satisfied with my location. Knowing that when I found the perfect office, I could relocate immediately was very appealing. However, a month-to-month lease is less secure than a longer term since you always run the risk of having the landlord rent it out to another tenant for more money, or for a longer term. You could also be subject to sudden rent increases.

If you are considering a month-to-month tenancy, you must beware that you could be getting set up. Back in my leasing days working for landlords, I prospected a retail tenant who was willing to move into the shopping center month to month only. I approached the landlord, who instructed me to proceed but also told me that in October I was to re-approach the tenant and give him 30 days' notice to sign a minimum three-year lease or vacate the premises. The landlord was willing to gamble that once the tenant spent a few months in the mall, set up shop, hired staff, and invested in signage, we could coerce him into signing the deal. Today, I am ashamed to admit I participated in this scheme. Unfortunately, it still happens, so be careful.

To avoid finding yourself in a similar situation, put a clause in your lease agreement that requires the landlord to give you three months' written notice of termination. You can also negotiate for a right of first refusal on any bona fide offers to lease the landlord may receive, or you might try negotiating for a short term, for example, one year, with a tenant's option to terminate with 30 to 90 days' notice. This way you are secure for one full year but can still get out of the agreement if need be.

Remember, landlords want cash flow, security, and quality tenants. Commercial brokers want large commissions that come from long term leases. There are, of course, landlords that will welcome you as a tenant, especially if the property has plenty of vacant space. Although a month-to-month lease agreement is usually cheaper than a long-term lease, to some landlords, the cash flow generated by month-to-month tenants is very attractive, even at only 50 percent to 80 percent of the asking price.

Your greatest obstacle may be overcoming the leasing broker who wants to hold the space for a prospective long-term tenant. If you come up against this obstacle, it is one of the few times when going above the leasing broker to the property manager or landlord makes sense. Most property managers are empowered to negotiate short-term or month-to-month lease agreements, and month-to-month arrangements are often easier to make if you are dealing directly with the landlord, in-house leasing representative, or property manager. If the broker has several tenants looking at leasing the same space the broker will often favor the tenant who wants the longest term since the end result in most cases will be a higher commission.

Naturally, a month-to-month tenant often has trouble negotiating for a relocation inducement, a tenant allowance, or free rent. However, you can often secure some tenant allowance money if you are willing to repay all or a portion if you terminate the lease before a specified time.

 A landlord and tenant can change anything in the lease agreement, anytime, as long as both parties agree to the change.

Month-to-month tenants who have occupied their premises for years have missed out on many freebies. You may wish to add a clause to your lease agreement that says that you, as tenant, will have months 13, 25, 37, and so on, free of minimum rent if you are still leasing the premises month to month at that time.

Some tenants who are planning to switch from a monthly arrangement to a long-term deal find it difficult to negotiate for any extras since they have already tipped their hand by admitting they want to stay. To avoid this possibility, you must do your homework by investing time locating alternative locations, and you must be prepared to consider moving if your landlord will not provide a competitive inducement package.

3. The Fixturing Period

The fixturing period immediately precedes the commencement date, which is the start date of the lease term. Typically, you will receive access to your premises 30 days before opening so that you can build out the space. This is the fixturing period.

It is important to negotiate several points about the fixturing period. First, the landlord must provide you with vacant possession of the premises. If you have leased a space that is currently occupied, the offer to lease should stipulate when you will receive vacant possession. This may or may not coincide with the start date of the fixturing period. For example, the offer to lease says that you will have vacant possession on May 1. But what if the current tenant hasn't moved out by that time? Or perhaps that tenant has moved out, but the landlord has not cleaned up the premises , replaced the ceiling, cleaned the carpets or done other landlord's work as agreed? It's best to give yourself some leeway.

It would be safer for you to state in the agreement that the fixturing period will begin five days after you, the new tenant, receive vacant possession of the premises.

Tenants often do not negotiate for a long enough fixturing period. But consider what would happen to your business if your contractor's materials are delayed, or your fixtures or office equipment don't arrive on time. In the 1980s, before I became active in commercial real estate, I opened a food court outlet in a shopping mall. All the tenants were scheduled to make a grand opening on the same day. However, my contractor didn't order the HVAC system early enough. It finally arrived and was installed six days late. Not only did I miss out on sales during my free rent period, but the lease agreement also contained a clause that stated there would be a $100-per-day penalty for late openings (which was fortunately not enforced). I encourage tenants to negotiate for a minimum 45 to 60-day fixturing period, or even as much as 90 days, to avoid unexpected delays. The key here is to be prepared. Try to have your space plan drawn and approved by the landlord before the fixturing period even starts. Get your contractor lined up and the building permit taken care of ahead of time, not during the fixture. I negotiated a five-month fixturing period for one of my clients but he still managed to open late due to poor planning. This resulted in him paying for rent in his old location as well as the new location simultaneously.

Another good clause to include in the lease agreement is one that states that the tenant will be permitted to open for business before the start date, gross-rent free. I negotiated this for one of my clients who was opening 20 retail outlets. Not only was he receiving six months of free rent, but he would often complete the build-out at least 30 days' before the lease start date. He was then able to open for business without paying any rent.

 Tenants are required to have their insurance in place when they take vacant possession of the premises, not just the day they open, so take care of this if you plan to open early.

Finally, the fixturing period should normally be gross-rent free. No minimum or base rent, no operating costs, and no promo or media funds should apply. Some landlords will try to make you pay rent or at least operating costs but don't be afraid to negotiate with them. If you are separately metered for utilities you may need to have these put in your company name on the first day of the fixturing period.

4. The Overholding Period

Suppose you come to the end of your lease term and do not have a new agreement, renewal, or extension in place. You will enter into what is called the overholding period. In itself the overholding period is not a problem. However, many lease agreements contain a clause that states that the tenant's rent will substantially increase during the overholding period. I have reviewed leases with built-in increases of up to 300 percent for the overholding period. A 50 percent to 100 percent increase is the industry standard. The overholding period is the landlord's way of preventing you from sitting back and remaining uncommitted about a renewal.

A tenant who wanted to relocate hired me to do her site selection. It took a while, but finally we found the perfect site. It took a while longer to negotiate a good deal with a ten-year term. By the time construction at the new site started, her existing lease had expired. The lease agreement for her current location called for the rent to increase to 200 percent of its original amount and the landlord was determined to enforce it. Fortunately, the tenant was able to move into a temporary location for two months while her new location was being constructed. Her old space remained empty for many months thereafter but the landlord took her move as a personal slight, thereby sacrificing two more months of rental income out of emotional spite.

After 22 years in the same location a well-known family owned bookstore owner hired me to do their site selection and relocate them. Even though a great location was found nearby, it would be several months before the new landlord could have the new location ready for my client to move in. As part of the inducement package I negotiated on the new location, we also included a condition that the new landlord would pay all overholding period penalty costs for my client at his old location while he waited to move in. This saved the tenant over $15,000, and just goes to show that if a landlord really wants your tenancy he or she will do whatever it takes to make the deal.

You must negotiate the overholding period from the outset. Ideally, you would negotiate for no increase at all; however, 10 percent to 25 percent is usually acceptable to the landlord.

5. Renewal Options

If you wish to sell your business before your lease ends, for instance, during year four of a five-year term, the renewal option and terms will be critical to the purchaser. Therefore, during your original lease negotiations you must include a renewal option or extension period. It is absolutely critical that the option be transferable to a landlord approved assignee (and not personal to you).

Try to avoid lease renewal options that won't allow the rent to go lower for the renewal period than its current amount. Or those that allow a renewal option only if, as a retailer, you have achieved percentage rent sales. Many leases have clauses which make any renewal option contingent on no further tenant allowance or free rent being paid. I have even seen leases that granted an option to renew on page 20 but later, for instance, on page 29, rescinded that option if the business was sold or the lease was assigned (transferred). As well, most leases say that if you are in default or have been in default (essentially, ever late with rent), the renewal option is nullified.

 Most lease renewal options are for a 5 year term — no more, no less. Build flexibility into your renewal option clause with the words "up to 5 years."

You will usually receive an option to renew your lease for a period equal to the original term. Therefore, if your first lease term is five years, the renewal option offered (if any) will also be for five years. However, be aware that this is negotiable. All you need to add to the clause in the lease agreement are the words "up to". A clause like, "The renewal period will be for a term of up to five years, as desired by the tenant," will ensure you the greatest flexibility. The tenant in the example above who was forced to rent temporary premises while her new premises were undergoing construction could have used this clause to extend or renew her lease for just two months.

Entrepreneurs approaching their senior years can use this flexible renewal option to coincide with retirement. Or suppose another landlord was constructing a better building or site across the street from you, but it would open eight months after your lease expired. By renewing for just eight months, you could make the relocation on your schedule.

I strongly encourage you not to let your lease renewal option become an afterthought. It is very difficult to negotiate a good lease renewal after four-and-a-half years of being in business because you didn't plan at the outset. Most landlords will grant multiple renewal options, especially if you are investing a lot of money on buildout of the premises or if you are a national franchiser or franchisee.

CHAPTER 5

NEGOTIATING STRATEGIES AND TACTICS

1. Find Out What Motivates Your Landlord

Landlords are motivated in various ways. The key to successful negotiating is learning what the other party wants. Did you know there are actually six classifications of landlords? These are —

(a) Institutional owners such as insurance companies

(b) Financial owners such as banks or savings and loan organizations

(c) Developers who construct, lease, and often sell properties

(d) Family owners who often purchase existing properties as long-term investments

(e) Investors who are absentee landlords, but somewhat similar to family owners in how they operate

(f) Partnerships, which are usually developers in partnerships with institutional or financial owners.

Insurance companies and banks own a lot of commercial property. They usually contract out the day-to-day management of each building. As you can imagine, they are driven by a different set of circumstances and objectives than landlords who are owners, managers, and perhaps even occupiers of small strip malls or office buildings.

An insurance company with deep pockets may want the tenant to have a strong covenant, demonstrated by being in business for many years, operating multiple locations, being a franchise or publicly traded company, and having a good credit rating, among other things. Since there is likely no mortgage on the building, cash flow is not as important to this type of landlord as it is to the local family-owned strip mall landlord. Sometimes, real estate developers, those companies that build, lease, and sell real estate projects as a business, will want to achieve very high face rents, so that the property value of the building is increased. Often such landlords will give generous build-out allowances and a lot of free rent to induce the tenant to sign at a high rent. This lets developers resell the buildings for much greater returns.

Unless you learn what objectives the landlord of a building has, you can't begin to maximize your negotiating position. So ask a lot of questions about the landlord before you even begin to deal. I frequently quiz the listing broker, especially if that is the person with whom I will be negotiating.

2. Negotiate for More Than You Expect to Get

Tenants often do not understand that in lease negotiations there is give and take. What you want and what you get are not always the same thing. Therefore it makes sense to open your lease negotiations by stating, offering, or asking for more than you need or expect to get. I use the word "asking" with some reservations since a good negotiator does not want to appear to be in a less powerful position by asking for anything. You should make an offer or state your requirements acting as the valuable customer you are.

Ask or negotiate for more than you expect to get and don't be afraid of rejection — that's all part of the way the game is played.

If you want four months of free rent, don't open negotiations asking for four months. You would be better off asking for seven months of free rent. To get one of my shopping center clients the maximum free rent, I told the leasing broker that we would need the first 18 months free. We negotiated and eventually settled at months 1 to 6 gross rent free and months 13 to 18 base/minimum rent free. If I had not gone after 18 months free I never would have gotten 12 months rent free.

If you are willing to pay $17 per square foot, make your initial offer approximately 20 percent lower, or for about $12 per square foot, and work up gradually if necessary.

Compromising is not negotiating. It's okay to compromise but recognize the difference. Let's say you offer to pay $10 per square foot rent, and the leasing broker counters your offer with $14. If you agree to pay the $14, you have neither negotiated nor compromised. If you counter offer at $12 or $13, you have compromised. If you offer $10.75, you are now negotiating. If you stick by your original offer, you are truly negotiating. And if you lower your offer to $9, you may be qualified to write a book like this one! Joking aside, remember that there is a time to compromise and a time to negotiate. However, if you are compromising all the time and kidding yourself into thinking you are negotiating, read this chapter twice.

Don't be afraid of rejection. If you need three parking stalls, ask for five. When I'm negotiating a lease or renewal for a client, I fully expect my first offer to be rejected. If my first offer is accepted, I may have let the tenant down by not asking for enough.

3. Negotiating to Win

When I interview tenants who are considering hiring me for consultation, I ask them what they expect to win in the negotiations. The majority deny even wanting to win. I have actually had tenants say to me, "Don't get me too good a deal or the landlord won't like me." Remember, landlords never sign deals they regret.

I spent many years leasing space for landlords before becoming a certified lease consultant and exclusively working for tenants. I was not judged solely by how many deals I made. The landlords considered many factors besides the rental rate, such as the strength or covenant of the tenant I brought in, the location and size of the premises leased, the term, and the presence of personal guarantees.

You are unlikely to negotiate a great deal if you are intimidated by the entire leasing process.

You must always negotiate to win the best lease terms: free rent, tenant allowances, more or cheaper parking, and so on. Even if it feels somewhat uncomfortable or unnatural, try to be proactive, not just reactive. If your negotiating skills need practice, experiment negotiating on things such as hotel room prices, car rental rates, and clothing purchases. If negotiating any of these less expensive items makes you uncomfortable, you need to practice your skills all the more. Once you get over the fear of rejection and being afraid to look like you can't afford something, you will begin to feel empowered by this new sense of control.

4. Be Prepared to Walk Away

You must always be fully prepared to leave the negotiating table. Many tenants find it difficult to walk away from a negotiation because they lack negotiating experience. Walking away is a negotiating tactic unto itself. If mastered, it will serve you well. But don't burn your bridges or let pride get in the way of returning to the bargaining table as circumstances change. Tenants with too much pride often miss opportunities.

Another reason you may find walking away from a deal difficult is because you have not done your homework. If you do not have information about other properties or leasing opportunities, you cannot effectively weigh one location against another.

Being able to walk away from a bad lease proposal is a strategy, one that will give you a tremendous feeling of empowerment once you have mastered it.

Tenants preparing to lease new premises often find themselves lacking in objectivity, especially after having invested days or even weeks in the process. The problem is compounded if they are running out of time to lease a space. Some tenants mistakenly spend thousands of dollars on space plans without even having an offer in place. Or perhaps a deposit has been made and is in jeopardy of being lost. In any of these circumstances, walking away from the negotiations is a difficult decision, but one you must be prepared to make if you want to get the best possible lease terms.

5. Watch What You Say

Watch what you say from the start. Everything you say and do will be scrutinized by the leasing broker. A few years ago, I recommended to a client that if he were asked by the leasing broker how much rent he was currently paying, to politely respond with, "No comment." My client admitted that had he been asked, he would have simply told the broker $14 per square foot. "Why shouldn't I tell the leasing broker what I'm paying at my current location?" he asked. I explained that since the space we were looking at was quite a bit lower in price we did not want to give the broker the idea that we were prepared to or even capable of paying more than need be. The point here is that if you volunteer too much information, or talk as if the deal is done, you will lose bargaining power.

Don't tip your cards when negotiating a lease; you will lose bargaining power.

Many years ago, before becoming a lease consultant, I was the manager of a shopping center. I was once contacted by the local telephone company for access to hook up someone's telephone line in the mall. However, the business owner who requested the line hookup was the prospective tenant who was still negotiating the lease with me at the time! Another time, a prospective tenant told some of our existing tenants and security personnel that she was moving into the building next month, yet we had not finalized all the lease terms. All concessions toward those tenants immediately stopped, because we knew that they had already decided to accept the offer or sign the lease without further negotiations. Tenants make this mistake far too often, resulting in higher rents, larger deposits, and less attractive terms than might have been negotiated, not to mention losing potentially free rent. Remember: What you say, and who you say it too, could come back to haunt you.

6. Give Smart Answers and Ask the Right Questions

The questions you ask and the answers you receive will greatly influence how you negotiate your lease. Usually, it's the leasing brokers who dominate preliminary discussions. Brokers are very good at asking questions that help them formulate pictures of your needs, strengths, weaknesses, vulnerabilities, and much more. Tenants are usually blissfully ignorant of how to properly answer loaded questions, or what they should be asking the brokers.

You will never receive the answers you need if you do not or cannot ask the right questions. Be sure to ask these questions:

(a) *Who is the landlord?* You can't always determine this just by looking at the building. If the landlord is an institutional owner, for example a pension fund or life insurance company, you will certainly negotiate the deal differently than if the property is a family operation owned and managed by a doctor and her son, where the doctor operates her medical practice right on the premises. As discussed earlier in this chapter, each of these types of landlords will have distinctive goals in owning that property.

(b) *Is the building for sale?* If the answer is yes, this is not necessarily a bad thing, but it will set the stage for a few more exploratory questions.

   (i) *When is the sale anticipated?* It is sometimes hard to close a lease deal if the buyer is in the due diligence stage.

   (ii) *Why is it being sold?* Is it for a healthy profit or because the property is yielding low returns? The leasing broker or landlord may not want to tell you this, but do try to find out — knowing will provide valuable insight for negotiating.

(iii) *Who is the buyer?* If the building has already been sold, the answer to this question could give you some insight to the type of landlord you will eventually be dealing with.

(iv) *Is the buyer planning any renovations or expansions?* Landlords will often plan renovations or expansions if they plan to buy the building. The costs incurred may eventually be charged back to the tenants through increased operating costs.

(c) *Who is the property manager?* Try to find out the caliber of property manager. Is he or she a certified property manager (CPM) or a real property administrator (RPA), or someone with little experience? You obviously want the highest qualified property manager possible.

(d) *Who were the last two tenants to move out of the building?* Once you have the answer to this question, you need to determine its implications. Did the tenants move up the street to better buildings, or did they go broke because of poor traffic to the building? Did the owners sell lucrative, thriving businesses, or did they simply retire?

(e) *Who were the last two tenants to move into the building?* Go and meet these tenants right away. Find out if they are happy with the landlord, the property manager, and their decisions to move in. Also inquire about what kind of lease deals they did, and whether they were paid their tenant allowance promptly. This is a critical step in your leasing process, so do not overlook it. Every building has a grapevine; failing to tap into this information will put you at a disadvantage.

(f) *What are the average annual sales?* This question is relevant to shopping centers and major strip malls. It is also a good idea to get the sales figures for your particular type of business.

(g) *What type of offer do you recommend?* Finally, ask the leasing broker what type of offer to lease he or she recommends you make. Take the recommendations with a grain of salt, but do not neglect to ask this question. The type of deal the broker indicates can be attained and what is put on paper as an offer to you can be greatly different. The opening written offer may be for appearances to the landlord and not a realistic expectation. Leasing brokers often know the landlord's preferences. These may include extra free rent to get the rental rate up, a high or low deposit, or a strong covenant.

When I talk about these questions at the seminars I give, someone eventually asks me if you can really expect to have your questions answered, and if so, how truthfully? First, be sure you are hearing the real answer. When the answer or response to your question is preceded by the words, "To the best of my knowledge," "I believe," "I think," or "It's likely that," be wary that you are being told only a partial truth. Ask for clarification and don't accept "I don't know" for an answer. Often the real answer you are searching for may be three or four questions deep. If you question the sincerity of the answer, and that answer is vital to your decision to lease that space, get the answer in writing as part of the offer to lease. Property managers and landlord brokers will not normally lie to a tenant. However, what you hear sometimes will be partial truths. For example, you ask if the grocery store that anchors the property is planning to move. The property manager, in an attempt to appease your concerns, tells you that the grocery store has a long term lease with many years yet to run. He did not answer your question since grocery stores have been know to move but keep paying their rent thereby honoring the lease agreement. You must ask good questions then listen carefully to the answer.

7. Have Someone Negotiate on Your Behalf

Ultimate authority is a problem most tenants encounter when negotiating lease agreements. Let's look at the landlord for a minute. There are usually one, two, or even three levels of management between the landlord (the decision maker) and the broker who is negotiating the lease. And there you are: you may be the company's president, number one employee, chief negotiator, and ultimate decision maker.

It is unlikely that you can change the landlord's method of doing business, but you can change yours. A few years ago, I sent my right-hand marketing representative out to flush out deals on a couple of properties for our own office space. He didn't know much about leases but made for a tremendous decoy. After he returned and reported his findings, we shortlisted and viewed a couple of buildings. I wrote what I wanted on a piece of paper and told him to get me those terms, conditions, and concessions. At that point, I think he was ready to quit my company: "There is no way we are going to get all of these things," he said. Nonetheless, back he went. Two days later after I had coached him along, we had a pretty good deal in place that I could step in and finish off.

Strategically place a partner, spouse, employee, or someone (without ultimate authority) at the leasing broker's level. Ideally you would want to hire a certified lease consultant to perform this service. This elevates you to the level of the landlord — truly the power position. After preliminary negotiations, you can step in.

Above all, remember that you are the customer. The rental money flows from you to the landlord, so take charge of your negotiations.

CHAPTER 6
NEGOTIATING OPERATING COSTS

Although operating costs are generally not negotiable, there is often more to them than meets the eye. By being aware of certain practices, you may be able to avoid paying more than you should.

Operating costs include items such as repair and maintenance of the asphalt in the parking lot, grass cutting, snow removal, property insurance, elevator maintenance and much, much more. In enclosed shopping centers, operating costs are called CAM (common area management) or maintenance. These costs are also referred to as occupancy costs. This will include common area costs such as cleaning, heating, and air-conditioning. You are usually required to pay whatever percentage of the overall building operating costs your premises occupy in that building. For example, if you occupy 10 percent of a building, you are generally required to pay 10 percent of the building's operating costs. If there is a cost associated with running the building the landlord will want to recover it from the tenants.

Your lease agreement will define the operating costs for the building. Operating cost definitions can vary widely in terms of detail. For example, if the operating cost definition lists landscaping as one item, this can mean almost anything to do with trees, shrubs, and grass! Some landlords use the landscaping clause to add thousands of dollars in trees to the property, and then charge this back to tenants as an operating cost. This type of scenario is discussed in more detail in section **6.**

Here are a few things to watch for to make sure you are getting the best deal possible.

1. Management Fees

It is a common industry practice for the landlord or property manager to charge a specified percentage or management fee on top of operating costs. The lease agreement usually states that the annual management fee is either 15 percent of the total annual operating costs or 5 percent of the tenant's annual gross rent, whichever is greater. For example, if the property manager pays $1,000,000 in operating costs for the year, he or she will charge you either an additional $150,000 in management fees or 5 percent of your gross rent, whichever is greater. However, already included in the million-dollar operating cost are salaries and benefits for all staff of the property manager. This means that the management company is double-dipping by charging a 15 percent management fee on the salaries of its own staff.

You can also see that there is no incentive to keep costs down since the more of the tenants' money the property manager spends on operating costs, the more he or she makes. If he or she is charging 5 percent of your rent as a management fee, this is also unfair to tenants paying higher rents but not necessarily enjoying more services or benefits. In many cases, such as property taxes and insurance, the 15 percent management fee is not justified since there is very minimal effort or work required to manage these expenses.

Although it is usually only tenants that are larger national companies that can successfully negotiate these management terms, it is still important for you to understand them.

2. Contractual Maintenance Services

Imagine that a property manager is tendering the yearly cleaning contract for a mid-size shopping center and receives three bids: $80,000, $90,000, and $110,000. All three companies are bidding on the same number of hours. Since the property manager's fee is 15 percent on top of what is spent, it is tempting for the property manager to take the higher quote.

But let's look at this scenario more closely. The difference in price may be explained this way: the lower bid will have several workers clean the building unsupervised each night. The second company operates in a similar way but includes a night supervisor who drops in periodically, hence the higher cost. The third company's quote includes a full-time supervisor on site each night to ensure top performance.

If the property manager hires the low-bidding company, he or she will make a management fee of $12,000 but will have to inspect the work each morning and deal with any problems. However, if the property manager hires the highest-bidding company, he or she will make $16,500, with supervision and management built into the cleaner's contract. This scenario also applies to landscaping, snow removal, and trash removal contracts.

Ideally, the property manager's contract should be based on incentives for spending less. Unfortunately, few are. While it is good for you to be aware of these types of contracting practices, do not invest your time searching for such a landlord or negotiating this point at length. There is little expectation of change to the status quo anytime soon.

3. Disproportionate Sharing of Operating Costs

There are a number of ways in which you can unknowingly pay more than your fair share of operating costs. By being aware of these pitfalls, you are empowered to negotiate your lease agreement in such a way as to avoid them.

First, be wary of a landlord or property manager who is handling several buildings where the same maintenance and management staff look after multiple properties. In one case I know of, the landlord of 19 buildings had a combined vacancy rate of 20 percent. However, 100 percent of the salaries of the property manager, administrative staff, and caretaker were being charged back to the tenants. If your lease agreement specifically states that the tenant will pay their proportionate share only, you should not be required to make up the shortfall because of those vacancies.

Make sure that 100 percent of operating cost chargebacks are warranted.

Here's another example of how you might end up paying more than you should. Suppose that you are a tenant in a 20,000-square-foot property. The manager for your building also manages a 40,000-square-foot building across town. The manager's annual salary is $40,000. The manager's salary should not be split in half and charged back to the buildings equally. Rather, the smaller building should be charged back one third, the larger building charged two thirds of the total salary and benefit package, etc.

When negotiating your lease, watch also for a lease clause that readjusts the proportionate share of each tenant's operating costs up to 95 or even 100 percent of the building's actual occupancy level. What this clause can mean is that as more spaces become vacant in your building or property, your percentage or proportionate share increases so that the landlord never has to absorb more than 5 percent of the actual operating costs. A tenant who came to me with this problem had been paying 17 percent of operating costs, since she occupied 17 percent of a fully occupied building. When one large tenant left, this woman's proportionate share of operating costs increased to 30 percent overnight. You can avoid this happening to you by negotiating to cap your operating cost increases to no more than 5 percent per year. Section **7.** below discusses capping operating cost increases in more detail.

With respect to utilities, separate metering is the only way to ensure that each tenant is being treated fairly. If tenants are not separately metered for utilities, a disproportionate share of these costs is usually charged back to them. For example, the hair salon may have 50 times the water consumption as the computer store next door, and the flower shop uses 5 times the power for its coolers as the clothing store. If your business consumes minimal utilities be sure that your premises are metered separately to avoid disproportionately paying another tenant's operating cost utilities.

4. Leasehold Improvements to Vacant Space

Landlords who manage their own properties are notorious for upgrading vacant units and charging the costs back to the tenants through operating costs. Sometimes it is no more than having the carpets professionally cleaned, but many times painting and actual leasehold improvements are conducted in order to make the space more leasable.

While this practice may seem fine when the landlord is doing these space upgrades for you, remember that if the landlord is doing these upgrades for you, he or she is likely also doing them for other tenants. Over time, you may be paying for these extras by way of higher operating costs.

You can hire a lease auditor or accountant to uncover these types of problems. Some lease agreements correctly specify that any expenditure represents a true recoverable operating cost only if it benefits all the tenants as a group and none of the tenants individually. This is a good clause to look for or have added to the lease agreement to prevent being charged for leasehold improvements to vacant space.

5. Penalty Fees for Late Payments

Some landlords who manage their own buildings regularly pay the operating cost bills late. Even though you and the other tenants may have paid your proportionate share of operating cost on time each month, the landlord may still delay paying the property taxes, trash removal bill, or parking lot repair company and incur penalty charges. Don't allow your landlord to pass these late fees or penalty charges on to you and the other tenants. It can be especially costly when property taxes are paid late.

Make sure your lease agreement explicitly states that the landlord may not include late payment penalty charges in the recoverable operating costs.

6. Amortized Operating Costs and Unamortized Capital Costs

Suppose your property manager spends $60,000 replacing the asphalt in the parking lot. Or suppose your landlord adds 12 new trees and shrubs to the front lawn and spends an additional $6,000 on landscaping. Or suppose the roof is replaced or a fancy new trash collecting area is constructed. These repairs and additions could be considered capital expenditures because they may theoretically add value to the building.

 Any legitimate operating cost should be amortized over the life of the upgrade, repair or replacement item.

Regular repair and maintenance is one thing, but if the value of the property increases as a result of the replacements or additions to the property, do not allow the landlord or property manager to automatically expense them as operating costs. And any legitimate operating cost should be amortized over the life of the upgrade. Using the example above, if the landlord does charge the asphalt or new trees back to the tenants, then the amounts should be spread over many years, not totally lumped into the current year. If your lease is expiring that year why should you pay for these long term benefits that you will not be around to enjoy?

There are many reasons why a property manager would want to charge back the entire cost of a replacement or addition to the property in just one year. One is that he or she can then get the full 15 percent management fee while he or she is still the property manager. If the landlord is managing his or her own building, it could be that he or she is unable to finance the cost of the work over many years, or that cash flow is tight because of vacancies or other distressed buildings owned by the same landlord.

Unfortunately, many tenants have signed lease agreements within which the landlord has cleverly constructed the operating cost clause to include capital expenditures. It really pays to use a magnifying glass when looking at the operating cost definitions in your lease agreement and negotiate accordingly for your protection. Look for the word "replacement" within the operating cost definitions, then negotiate to change it to the words "repair or maintain." You should expect the landlord to maintain the heating, ventilation, and air-conditioning (HVAC) system with scheduled preventive maintenance, thereby avoiding replacement of the HVAC system and other expensive items.

As mentioned in the introduction to this chapter, another term to watch out for is "landscaping." Replace this word with elaborations such as "services to existing greenery, including grass cutting, fertilizing, weeding, pest control, watering...tree and shrub maintenance, excluding the addition of a sprinkler system or permanent tree beds or pots."

7. Capping Operating Cost Increases

The best way to estimate whether a property will undergo substantial operating cost increases is to look at the operating costs for the past few years. Increases up to 5 percent per year in operating costs should be budgeted for by the tenant as inflationary.

Ask, and if necessary demand, what the actual operating costs have been for the past three years. If the increases have averaged, for example, 4.5 percent each year, they will likely remain constant, increasing by the same amount for the next three years.

If the increase is, for example, 12 percent in one particular year, such a high increase is usually an indication of a capital expenditure masked as an operating cost, or an indication that costs are not being amortized over the full number of life years, or that proper upkeep wasn't done to the property in past years, and this is a catch-up year.

The longer you look to the past for a history of operating costs increases, the further into the future you can project increases.

If you notice that the property is looking run down or the property manager or owner is changing, this could affect the operating costs for the future. Increases to operating costs, anywhere from 50 percent to 100 percent, are common in older buildings that have undergone multi-million dollar renovations. Many lease agreements anticipate and allow for renovation costs (whether capitalized or not) to be charged back to tenants as part of their operating costs, so before you sign an offer to lease, take time to check this issue out, especially if the building is older and potentially prime for renovating and/or expanding.

Approximately 75 percent of landlords have no problem capping yearly operating cost increases to a maximum of 5 percent, although some insist that the cap apply only to controllable costs. A property tax increase, for example, would not be within their control.

8. Hiring a Lease Auditor

Lease audits or, more appropriately, operating cost audits, became commonplace a few years ago. Tenants who want to check up on their landlords by having the property operating costs audited or analyzed can now easily do so. Many major cities have someone who specializes in audits and space measurements.

A lease auditor will do two main things for the tenant. First, in reviewing the expenditures, the auditor will determine if the cost was truly recoverable as an operating cost or expense, or whether the landlord was charging back to tenants costs that were not agreed to in the lease. Such costs often include landscaping and leasehold improvements to vacant space, and occasionally broker commissions.

Second, the auditor will determine if the expenditures were reasonable. In one case I was involved with, the auditor revealed that the property manager was charging the costs of the building's paper recycling program back in operating costs. Not only did the operating cost clause within the lease agreement not include paper recycling, but we learned that many paper recyclers would actually pick up and buy scrap paper and cardboard from tenants and landlords, as opposed to the tenants having to pay the recycler to haul it away.

Recently, I performed an operating cost audit for a group of tenants. Over $80,000 in discrepancies were revealed and the landlord was forced to make the necessary adjustments due to my findings. Now the tenants are more on guard than ever to ensure they are fairly treated.

Take time to review the operating cost clause definition within the formal lease agreement before signing the offer to lease and when you review the formal agreement itself. Talk to some of the other tenants in the building. If they are already disgruntled with the landlord or property manager's practices, in all likelihood you will be too.

CHAPTER 7
NEGOTIATING THE RENTAL RATE

Imagine that before beginning a lease negotiation, you knew what every other tenant in the building was paying for rent. You knew which tenants were month to month and which were planning to move out. Suppose you also knew which tenants were paying their rent on time and which weren't. Would this information enable you to negotiate more confidently? Of course it would. Any person with this information would have an advantage in the negotiating process. Now consider that the landlord's leasing brokers and property manager, and even outside brokers, either have or can gain access to this information directly from the landlord.

Having "inside" information allows leasing brokers to negotiate with a greater sense of certainty, thereby giving the leasing advantage to the landlord's broker. Make sure you get the "inside" information, too!

Many landlords do not charge the same rent per square foot consistently from one tenant to another. It is not uncommon for two tenants with identical spaces to be paying rental rates that differ by as much as 50 percent to 100 percent. Some tenants would have also received incentive packages and others practically nothing at all. Therefore you must level the negotiating field by doing your homework and getting all the information you can. In one lease renewal negotiation that I am working on right now, the landlord is dictating that the tenant's rent must increase by $2 to $3 per square foot over the five year renewal term. However, my investigations clearly show that every other tenant in the strip mall is paying less rent than my client (who negotiated his first lease on his own). If the landlord does not now lower the tenant's rent we will go to arbitration confident of a victory.

1. How Is the Rental Rate Set?

Rental rates are set by landlords so as to service their mortgages and make reasonable profits. Contrary to what many tenants believe, rental rates have nothing to do with how much rent landlords think tenants can reasonably pay. This is a point you cannot afford to miss.

In a hot market, landlords may raise their rents, or, conversely, drop them in a cold one. If you question leasing brokers as to how they came up with a particular rental rate, they will more than likely reply that they are simply asking the market rate. This can be misleading depending on which set of variables you use. In many cases market rates do not apply to retail buildings. They will apply however to office buildings and industrial sites. This is because in retail, two tenants side by side may have dramatically different rental rates — the market is unpredictable. Tenants of office and industrial space usually have deals similar to their neighbors', and so market rates are a reliable basis for calculating what a rental rate should be for them.

When looking at retail space, be sure to investigate what the prevailing rental rate is, rather than the market rent.

If you are looking for retail space, you should be most interested in the prevailing rate. The prevailing rental rate is reflected in the last few deals done at a property. Tell the leasing broker that you need information on these last few deals and not just on rental rates.

If you are negotiating a lease on office or industrial space, you can confidently look to past lease deals to determine what is a fair market value. Once this information is gathered, you must decide on your negotiating strategy. Do you decide that you are not willing to pay more than the last tenant? Or that you want to pay 15 percent less than the last tenant?

The rental rate, of course, is only one component of the deal to be negotiated. However, if the rental rate is critical to your business, you must set a realistic figure that you are willing to pay and then start your negotiations at least 20 percent below that figure.

It is not uncommon for a landlord to buy-up the minimum rental rate with free rent incentives or cash inducements. One landlord for whom I leased space before becoming a lease consultant wanted to achieve minimum $10 rental rates to create a particular paper value for the property plus a positive cash flow. The prospective tenants interested in leasing the space were willing to pay only $7 per square foot. The landlord induced the tenant into signing a five-year lease by buying up the deal. The landlord gave the tenant $3 per square foot in cash or free rent for the entire term above and beyond the regular incentives. Landlords sometimes insist that these inducements be excluded from the actual lease agreement but stipulated in a side agreement. This way they can try to avoid showing the mortgage holder, other tenants, or potential buyers of the property how they achieved such good rental rates.

Getting correct information on what landlords are receiving for a net effective rental rate (discussed in more detail in section **5.** below) is not easy. You may have to talk with the leasing broker, the property manager, and a few tenants in the building to determine what the prevailing rental rate really is.

Do you remember the discussion on what motivates different types of landlords? Knowing what type of landlord you are dealing with and what his or her motivating factors are will help you determine to a great extent how the rental rate is being set, and how firm or flexible the landlord will be on it.

2. Let the Landlord Make the First Offer

It is a common negotiating blunder for tenants to make the first offer to lease, or to make an offer to renew their lease before the landlord makes them an offer. Would you walk up to a house builder and offer $225,000 before even seeing the sticker price? Of course not. Yet, most tenants, over a five-year lease term, pay much more rent than the cost of a new house. Earlier this year, I addressed about 200 store owners who were part of a national chain. They had all come into town for a three day convention and I had been invited to speak to them about how to become better lease negotiators. The group was very attentive and responsive to my message and questions. Since almost everyone was from out of town and staying in hotels I asked them who had called the hotel before arriving and booked their room by offering to pay a particular price for the room. No one raised their hand because no one would do this. You would want to know what the hotel is charging before even offering them a lower rate wouldn't you. Well the same analogy applies to commercial lease negotiating.

Not only should you let the broker or landlord be first to make the offer, but you should also get this first offer in writing. Don't accept a verbal quote. There is a lot of room for misunderstanding and disagreement if you don't have anything on paper. Once you have received their offer, you can make a calculated, bona fide counter offer to the landlord. This can be done by making handwritten changes to the offer and signing it back, or it can be completely rewritten.

3. Beware of Inflated Offers

Beware of inflated offers. These words of advice can't be said too often. Earlier in this book, I described tenants who accepted offers from leasing brokers or the landlord without even trying to negotiate better terms. They did not realize that the leasing broker or landlord expected to negotiate down. This lesson is so important that it bears repeating in this chapter on negotiating the rental rate.

Before becoming a lease consultant and working exclusively for tenants, I worked for landlords. I once leased a property on behalf of its landlord where the asking rental rate was $18 per square foot. If potential tenants telephoned or walked into the office, I would quote the $18 rate. More often than not, any deal on the premises would get down to a range of $13 to $15 per square foot, which was all the landlord really expected anyway. Every so often, however, a prospective tenant who had not done his or her homework would agree to the $18 rental rate. These tenants are not aware that the leasing broker's first offer is usually inflated to achieve the actual desired rental rate. Such an offer also serves to create the illusion of a win-win deal, where both parties negotiated to some middle ground.

Years later, working as a lease consultant, I was hired to negotiate a tenant's new lease. The landlord was asking $8 per square foot and I negotiated the deal down to $1 per square foot escalating to $3 per square foot over a five year term. Since my client was leasing over 14,000 square feet the saving were incredible. So beware of inflated offers from the landlord.

4. Consider the Square Footage

The size or area of the premises and those in close proximity greatly determine the rental rate, especially in retail settings. For example, a 1,200-square-foot unit directly adjacent to a 2,800-square-foot unit may be priced by 50 percent more per square foot than the larger space depending on certain other variables. Recently, a shopping center leasing broker quoted a minimum rent of $48 per square foot on a 545-square-foot unit just two doors down from a 1400-square-foot unit priced at $23 per square foot. This occurs because products and pricing vary. The smaller store may actually do a higher volume of sales than the larger store. The landlord will want to maximize rental income and therefore charges accordingly. Unfortunately, there is not much you can do about this practice; it is generally accepted in the industry.

Leasing brokers will usually be more motivated to lease larger units than smaller units. This means that when you are presented with a number of units to choose from, you will usually be better off by looking at smaller units first. If you show interest in or even negotiate on a larger unit first — that is, a unit larger than the size you want — and then show interest in a smaller unit — that is, a unit the size you want — the leasing broker will likely jack up the rent per square foot on the smaller unit even more than usual in an attempt to persuade you to lease the larger space. However, if you begin by negotiating on a unit that is smaller than one you want, and then ask for prices on larger units, you will likely get a better overall rental deal, since the leasing broker will want you to take the larger space.

5. Calculating Net Effective Rent (NER)

It is important for you to understand that what you pay the landlord in rent isn't always what it seems. The term net effective rent (NER) refers to the actual rent value the landlord receives after deducting the expenses associated with doing the deal. These costs include items such as real estate commissions, free rent, and the tenant allowance, landlord's work etc. So the rent you've agreed to pay might be $8 per square foot, but after calculating and deducting the costs above, the net effective rent might be closer to $5.95 per square foot.

It is important for you to understand this so that when you negotiate your lease renewal, you do not automatically agree to continue to pay what you paid in the past. If the prevailing rate has remained relatively stable since you first negotiated your original lease, and you don't receive any inducements or allowances for the renewal term, theoretically your rent should go down to $5.95 per square foot for the renewal term. Inflation can play a factor in rental increases, but generally only to a limited extent.

6. Graduated or Stepped Rent

Another strategy to consider when negotiating your rental rate is graduated, escalated, or stepped rent. One landlord I was negotiating a commercial lease deal with on behalf of a client was insisting on receiving $14 per square foot for the full five-year term. After implementing the strategies in this book, the tenant and I closed the deal with a stepped rent provision. Here is how it worked: Rent for year 1 was $9 per square foot, year 2 was $10, year 3 was $11, year 4 was $12, year 5 was $13, and years 6 through 10 was $14 per square foot. This type of graduated rent saved the tenant a lot of money. The net effective rental rate for the first five years was just $11 per square foot, substantially lower than the $14 being asked.

The landlord, had he been in a stronger position, could have negotiated to step the rent this way: year 1 at $9, year 2 at $13, year 3 at $14, year 4 at $15, and year 5 at $19 per square foot. This would have netted an effective rent of his original asking price of $14 per square foot, less any other costs or inducements.

If you want a graduated rental plan, sometimes starting below the asking price and going above it, as illustrated in the preceding example of what the landlord might have obtained, is the only way. However, I encourage you to negotiate so the rent for the last year of your term does not exceed, or even comes slightly short of, the landlord's asking rent.

If you are negotiating with a sophisticated leasing broker or landlord, he or she may insist on a stepped rent starting at the asking rate. This is because the $14 will not be worth the same in ten years' time, because of inflation. While this may be true, you don't have to let this sway your negotiating decisions. Remember, you must be prepared to walk away from a deal you're not happy with.

7. Offer to Pay Higher Rent

Another strategy to consider when negotiating rent is to offer to pay higher rent. Naturally, every tenant wants to pay the least rent possible. But rent may in fact be only a small component of your total overhead. To help with other, more immediate costs, you may want to pay higher rent, but get immediate cash back

— a kind of rebate — from the landlord. Suppose you are leasing 2,500 square feet for a five-year term. Every dollar per square foot equals $12,500 of minimum rent over the lease term ($2,500 x 5 years). Now, let's say you have negotiated an $11-per-square foot rental rate. You could then offer to pay $3 per square foot more over the term, that is, $14 per square foot. This would net you a cash allowance equivalent to the rental value of $37,500 (the difference between the total rent at $11 per square foot and that at a $14-per-square-foot rate).

Often, if tenants can justify to landlords their need for the additional cash allowance, for example, for leasehold improvements or equipment purchases, they will receive all or at least a portion of the money requested. Landlords often offer this type of buy-up in partial or free rent, to avoid paying cash. For many tenants, receiving 6 months of free rent and the balance of $18,750 in cash is workable also. Don't hesitate to be creative. Negotiating free rent is discussed in chapter **8.**

However, be cautious when negotiating to pay a higher rent. Once you have spent the buy-up money, you will be stuck with those higher rent payments for a long time. As well, your business might be more difficult to sell since prospective buyers will take the higher rent into consideration when valuing the business.

8. Remember to Flinch

Flinching is an old but very effective negotiating strategy. Be prepared to flinch when the leasing broker quotes you a rental rate. Try to sound and look amazed or perhaps bewildered or in disbelief that anyone would actually pay the amount quoted.

Follow your best flinch with these words: "Well, you must be offering a tremendous incentive package to get that rate. What does it include?" By doing this, you are inviting the leasing broker to offer inducements such as free rent and tenant allowance money.

Don't be concerned about looking like you can't afford the space. The reason so many people refuse to flinch when they hear a price quote is pride. The other reason is ignorance. As I mentioned in chapter **5**, you must get over such a fear in order to be empowered in your negotiations.

The rental rate for your leased premises is usually second in importance to the site selection. However, for some landlords, the rental rate is first in importance. (Again, this depends on which type of landlord you are dealing with; that is, on what motivates your landlord in a leasing deal.) Typically you should make your first offer 20 percent to 25 percent lower than the asking rate. Don't be surprised if the leasing broker sounds taken aback: professional negotiators know the importance of flinching, too.

Remember that negotiating a good deal takes time and is not necessarily easy. I made this comment at one of my recent speaking engagements. One member of the audience responded by saying that his lease renewal negotiations always went quite smoothly, and that he found negotiating in general to be fairly easy. I had to surmise that if that were so, he was likely leaving a lot on the table during those negotiations. I can tell if I've negotiated hard enough the same way I can tell if I've played my hardest at tennis: I'm physically drained and emotionally satisfied that I did all that could be done. Don't be afraid to take a few bumps and bruises along the negotiating path. Your goal isn't to make friends with your landlord but to secure the best lease deal possible.

CHAPTER 8
NEGOTIATING FREE RENT

Probably the most unpredictable but most interesting part of the lease agreement that I negotiate is the free rent period. Some landlords or their leasing brokers are quite flexible when it comes to free rent but others are not so liberal. In one ten-year lease deal that I negotiated for a doctor I was able to get the tenant the first four years minimum rent free. For another tenant I got 18 months free plus a $180,000 tenant allowance. On a lease renewal negotiation we frequently negotiate for free rent and get it, which totally astounds some tenants who didn't even get free rent on their first lease term.

Free rent on lease renewals is often achievable and not unreasonable in some situations — if you know what buttons to push with the landlord.

Savvy leasing brokers will often offer rental rates that assume that a certain amount of free rent will have to be asked for by the tenant. If you do not negotiate for that free rent, if you leave it on the table, you have lost the free rent that was waiting for you.

Often, the incentive package is made to artificially raise the rental face rate. Most landlords would prefer to make a $15-per-square foot deal than a $12-per-square-foot deal, since the former will dramatically improve the property value of the building.

1. Negotiate for More Than You Expect to Get

During my last year as a commercial leasing broker working for landlords (before I became a lease consultant), I represented an absentee landlord who had a small strip mall in my city. One day a woman walked into the building's leasing office to inquire about leasing space there. After asking her a few questions, I was able to determine that she had not looked elsewhere in the community. She liked our building for several reasons and she had never operated her own business before. I began by giving her a tour of the building. Knowing that she was inexperienced and already emotionally attached to the property, I offered her our standard rental deal, including one month of free rent (the landlord's bare minimum).

Wisely, she consulted with her lawyer before making a decision. The lawyer suggested she ask for two months of free rent. Without hesitation she signed an offer to lease and made a large deposit. Within two days the landlord accepted the offer and the deal was quickly closed.

In one way, the tenant had done well by negotiating the free rent period up from one month to two. What she did not know was that I (as the landlord's agent) had been preauthorized by the landlord to give up to six months of free rent if necessary to close the deal. Why did the tenant not get more free rent? Simply because she did not ask for it.

Free rent is the easiest concession for a landlord to make. As a general negotiating rule, always ask or negotiate for more free rent than you need or want. This is especially pertinent if the premises are vacant and have been for some time. Aim for at least one month of free rent for each year of your term. But, remember to begin negotiations at more than that. If you begin negotiations at five months' free rent, the leasing broker may negotiate you down to three months. If you are signing a five-year lease, open negotiations at nine months' free rent, and be prepared to back down to five months.

I was able to get 12 months of free rent for one of my retail clients. I opened negotiations insisting on 18 months of free rent. Was it a gutsy thing to do? Of course, but what have you really got to lose. Remember to ask and negotiate for more than you expect to get.

2. Spreading Out the Free Rent

For new startup businesses landlords may have reservations about giving too much free rent. One strategy to calm a landlord's concerns that your business may not make it and have to close prematurely is to spread out the free rent over time. Suppose you want the first six months of minimum rent free, but the landlord will agree to give you only two months. You should counter offer still insisting on six months but offering to take the free rent over a longer period of time. For example, you could take months 1, 2, 13, 25, 37, and 49 free, rather than consecutively all up front. Or you might want to agree to receive the free rent applied to every second month of the term. Month 1 is free free, month 2 rent is due, month 3 rent is free, and so on. I did this for a daycare client getting here 18 months of free rent (every 2nd month free) over a 36 month period. As you can see, there is no absolute formula for negotiating free rent you just need to be creative.

Consider other combinations as well. For example, you could try to negotiate 12 months of free rent — the first 6 months gross free and then months 13 through 18 minimum rent free. Gross rent is discussed below. This will give the landlord some cash flow and ease their concerns about your going out of business in the first year after having received so much free rent up front.

3. Free Minimum Rent versus Gross Rent

As discussed in chapter **5,** on negotiating strategies, landlords should be responsible for paying operating costs for all spaces in their buildings, even when that space is vacant. If a building is 20 percent vacant, the landlord must still pay that 20 percent of the property taxes, utilities, and general operating costs. Some leases may have exceptions or exclusions to this general rule, but in most cases, vacant space actually costs the landlord money.

Should you negotiate for gross rent free (minimum rent and operating costs) or minimum rent only? By negotiating for minimum rent free, which means you pay operating costs from the first day, you will be a more attractive tenant to landlords. Although a landlord will receive no minimum rent from you for several months, he or she won't be paying the operating costs out of his or her pocket, either.

What you should concentrate on is getting the highest dollar value in free rent. In most cases 6 months of free minimum rent will have a higher value to the tenant than say 3 months of gross rent free anyway so be flexible.

4. Negotiate Half Rent Free

Some landlords are very concerned with achieving certain rental rates on paper but have no problem making other concessions. Suppose you want seven months of free minimum rent but the landlord will give you only three months free. Rather than concede your position, you might counter propose that months 4, 5, 6, and 7 be half rent free; that is, that you pay only half the agreed upon monthly rent. A surprising number of landlords will agree to this proposal, and it is an especially good strategy for a new business that needs some start-up time to get established.

You may even be able to get the first five months of minimum rent free and the rest of the first year at half rent. If you are trying to negotiate this, suggest that it be written as a separate condition or concession rather than as actually lowering the rental rate per square foot value. This allows the landlord to have their full rental rate showing on paper, while you get the concession anyway.

5. Cashing In Your Free Rent

You may at some time in your business find it's necessary to raise capital. If you have negotiated a free rent period for your lease agreement, it may be possible for you to exchange that free rent for cash. Here again, the better you can justify your need for the money to your landlord, the more likely you are to get it.

If your rent is $3,000 per month and you have five months free, the cash value is $15,000. However, because it means an outlay of cash for the landlord, he or she may want you to discount this cash value by up to 20 percent. You will have to weigh the pros and cons of your particular situation to determine if cashing in free rent minus a discount for the landlord still makes sense for you and your business.

6. Extend the Lease Term

If you are negotiating for substantial free rent (or any other benefits), the leasing broker may claim that the net effective rate is too low. If you run into this argument, consider agreeing to lease the space for a longer term or period of time.

It is not uncommon to extend the lease term by two months to cover the landlord's cost of paying the leasing broker's commission. A five-year lease would then become a 62-month lease term. Here again creativity in the negotiating process can benefit both parties. Above all, remember to take your time and do your homework. Doing so will always pay off.

If you are reading this book to prepare yourself to negotiate a lease renewal, try to find out what incentives the landlord is giving new tenants who are moving into the building. If new tenants are getting free rent, then why shouldn't you also?

As a final word I will speak to those business owners who have failed to get free rent on their new lease or their lease renewal. If you have struck out — and some of you will have — it is either the result of an inflexible landlord who is in an all-powerful position or your personal lack of negotiating skills. In most cases it will be the latter problem. Over 90 percent of my clients opening a new business get substantial free rent packages. On lease renewal negotiations approximately 75 percent of my clients receive free rent. After negotiating her heart out on a lease for a new location a franchisee turned to me for help. I was able to persuade the landlord to give her twice as much free rent (plus other inducements) as he had originally agreed to. Negotiating for free rent is an unpredictable at best.

CHAPTER 9
NEGOTIATING THE TENANT ALLOWANCE OR LEASEHOLD IMPROVEMENTS

While most tenants and even some leasing brokers make no distinction between a tenant allowance and leasehold improvement work done by the landlord, they are very different. Depending on my client's circumstances, I will often recommend one over the other for the reasons outlined in this chapter. The following information will help you determine which method will provide you with the best results.

For tenants renewing their lease agreement and who require upgrades or cosmetic renovations, you will almost always opt for a tenant allowance rather than have the landlord do the work for you. This is, of course, assuming that you are successful in negotiating a tenant allowance on your renewal term.

1. Tenant Allowance

The premises you are about to lease (or that you currently occupy) will often require some form of renovations or build-out. If you decide to negotiate for a tenant allowance you will be required to coordinate all aspects of the construction project. It could be as simple as getting a quote for new carpet or so detailed that professional design drawing will be required, taking into consideration specific electrical and plumbing requirements.

Most lease agreements state that the tenant allowance is a predetermined amount of money that the landlord will pay to the tenant after satisfactory completion of the work. Most lease agreements also require other conditions be met before the tenant is paid the tenant allowance. First, the tenant must be open for business. Second, the formal lease agreement is completely executed. Third, the tenant has had the contractor provide a statutory declaration proving there are no sub-trade liens on the building, and that everyone who worked on the project has been paid. Fourth, all of the construction work has indeed been completed and the cost of the work at least equaled the amount of the tenant allowance. The allowance is generally payable 45 days after the tenant's compliance with these three requirements, since any contractors or sub-trades will have 45 days to file a lien on the property if they have not been paid.

Because you will not be reimbursed by the landlord until the work is complete, you will either need enough money up front or you will need to arrange for a bridge loan from the bank. It's important to note that some landlords will actually make progress payments on the tenant allowance. I have frequently negotiated for my clients to receive one-third of the money upon signing the offer to lease. Another third is then paid when half of the project is completed. The balance is often paid out within two weeks after the project is completed. Many landlords will insist on paying the tenant allowance jointly to both you and the contractor to ensure the money gets into the right hands. This policy is not necessarily a reflection on your tenancy but on previous deals gone astray for the landlord.

 Some landlords will partially advance your tenant allowance, especially if you allow them to pay it directly to the contractor.

Cost overruns, poor workmanship, and completion delays are all part of the potential problems involved when you coordinate the renovations or build-out yourself. If you are trying to get your new business set up, it could be more stress than you want, so think carefully about whether negotiating a tenant allowance is the right route for you.

Choosing a tenant allowance over leasehold improvements gives you greater control over the project, and if you bring the project in under budget, the unspent funds will usually be converted into free rent if you negotiated for this consideration in advance.

At the time of writing this book and for several years before, most of North America was a renters' market. Consequently, I usually was able to negotiate tenant allowances for my clients equal to 100 percent — or more — of the work that needed to be done. Naturally, rental markets and times change but at the time of writing this revised version I still feel most of North America is a renters' market if you are prepared to do your homework, so do the best you can!

1.1 Ensuring you are paid

Once you have negotiated a tenant allowance, you need to ensure that you actually receive it.

If you are negotiating a tenant allowance, consider including a "what if" clause in your lease agreement to protect you if the landlord doesn't pay it.

There are various reasons why tenants don't receive their tenant allowance as stipulated in the lease agreement. Perhaps the landlord goes into receivership. In once such case a tenant invested $45,000 of his own money into leasehold improvements and expected to be fully reimbursed by the landlord who had agreed to pay a $45,000 tenant allowance. When the landlord went broke before paying the tenant allowance, it became a nightmare for the tenant. In another case the landlord simply claimed to be broke but still owned the property. The tenant's recourse turned out to be legal action.

One large landlord was notorious for not paying its tenant allowances. Typically the tenant would be encouraged by the landlord to take free rent in lieu of the allowance. While this is better than not getting paid at all, it will normally cause the tenant all sorts of other financing problems that were not anticipated. To fully protect yourself, include a "what if" clause in your lease agreement such as: "If the landlord does not pay the tenant allowance, the tenant may opt to take 150 percent of the tenant allowance value in free gross rent." This is a big incentive to landlords to pay the allowance since you would now receive 50 percent more value.

If the landlord balks during negotiation at including such a clause, ask him or her for the names of the last three tenants who were paid allowances, and then do your homework by talking to those tenants.

1.2 Charging tax on tenant allowance

Imagine that you have moved into your new premises or renovated your existing location and your tenant allowance check for $60,000 arrives. Your accountant will expect you to remit a percentage of the allowance, often amounting to thousands of dollars, to cover federal, provincial, and/or state taxes. But you forgot to charge the tax to the landlord!

Whenever you negotiate tenant allowance, make sure the lease agreement states the amount to be paid plus any applicable federal or state/provincial taxes. While it may be possible to recover the tax after-the-fact from your landlord, it is of course much simpler to include the tax clause right up front in the offer to lease and make no assumptions. It could mean a saving of thousands of dollars!

Remember to invoice your landlord for the tenant allowance sooner rather than later. Tenants often wait for weeks or months to receive their allowance when the landlord is waiting to be invoiced. On the invoice specify to whom or to what company you want the payment to be made, and any applicable taxes mentioned above.

2. Leasehold Improvements

Whenever you make an offer to lease, you can negotiate for the landlord to build-out the space, lay the new carpet, paint the walls, and do other such leasehold improvements for you. The landlord will tender the project and turnkey the premises, but only to the extent predetermined in the clause called "Landlord's Work." You will need to select color schemes and pick window coverings, as well as attending to the other decisions, but all responsibilities, including delivering the premises to you on time, will be the landlord's. Since the landlord will also be using his or her own money to finance the project, having the landlord complete the leasehold improvements can be a lot simpler for you than waiting to be paid a tenant allowance.

 Create a wish list of leasehold improvements. Then negotiate for them in your offer to lease.

Because the cost of leasehold improvements is calculated into your minimum/base rent (for example, you can choose between paying $6 per square foot with no improvements and $8 per square foot with improvements done by the landlord), you must watch out for landlord-inflated prices. Some landlords even own a construction company just to do build-outs, since it can be very profitable. I have seen landlords' contractors not only exaggerate and inflate construction costs but also deliver less than promised. In one case, the landlord agreed to install a 28 ounce carpet but instead installed an inferior 18 ounce carpet expecting that the tenant wouldn't notice. This saved the landlord over one thousand dollars over the quoted price. Sometimes, walls get painted only once, rather than twice. Second-hand store grill doors and other materials from around the building are sometimes substituted for new materials. Consider having your offer to lease stipulate that the project will be tendered to three construction companies. And that you have the right to approve the construction company awarded the construction project, regardless of cost. After all, it's not just price but quality of workmanship that matters. This should protect you from shoddy work and price padding.

3. Paying for Your Own Improvements to Minimize the Rental Rate

Occasionally tenants (usually professionals) will want to minimize their rental rate by paying for the leasehold improvements themselves. If you are considering this, it is important to ensure that you are actually saving money through reduced rent, not simply foregoing the benefit of receiving a tenant allowance or leasehold improvement.

For my clients who have the money to pay for the improvements and want the lowest rental rate possible, I usually negotiate up-front for all the inducements and allowance money that I can get for the tenant. Then I trade or exchange down for a lower rent. This way I am sure we ultimately got the lowest rent possible.

CHAPTER 10
NEGOTIATING THE LEASE DEPOSIT

Very few tenants actually negotiate their lease deposit, yet it is often quite negotiable. Just two months ago, a tenant in Virginia hired me to negotiate her lease deal. The landlord was insisting on a $60,000 deposit and I was able to negotiate that down to just $14,000.

The industry standard security deposit is first and last months' minimum/base rent (rent not including operating costs or taxes). All too often I hear of tenants who have agreed to pay ridiculous amounts of deposit. One naive tenant was persuaded by a landlord to pay a four-month deposit — the first two months of minimum rent and the last two months of minimum rent. Another tenant who was renewing his lease for the third consecutive five year term was being forced to make a security deposit even though he had never missed or been late with a rent payment. Since landlords rarely pay interest on deposits it's worth your while to negotiate hard.

In a few isolated situations you can turn the landlord's greed to your advantage. By offering a larger than normal deposit you may be able to win a particular location over a competitor or secure a good inducement package.

If money is tight, you should avoid saying or implying that you don't have sufficient funds for a deposit, since this will make you appear to be a high risk to the landlord. It is okay to say you won't put up a deposit, but obviously less effective to say you can't put up a deposit.

1. The Real Reason for a Deposit

Rarely is a deposit large enough to make the difference between whether a tenant fulfills the lease obligation or not. If a tenant is going broke, a $2,200 deposit won't stop the tenant from closing or make any significant difference to the landlord's financial position.

The real reason for the deposit is to offset the leasing broker's commission. Usually, the first and last month's rent roughly equates to whatever commission the landlord has agreed to pay out to leasing brokers. If the leasing broker doesn't get the tenant to cough up a deposit with the offer to lease, the landlord will have to dig into his or her own bank account to pay the leasing broker's commissions.

The deposit is also a closing tool used by leasing brokers who know that the average tenant doesn't have enough money to make a deposit on more than one property. By getting a deposit from you, the leasing broker knows he or she will not likely lose the tenancy to another leasing broker who may also showing you space elsewhere.

Leasing brokers usually have many deals on the go at the same time. For the sake of appearances, listing rights, and even monetary advances, it is to their benefit to have many deals, including yours, at the deposit stage.

Don't be fooled into thinking that if you have a deposit on a space, you are first in line or have some legal priority to that location. While some brokers may give you this courtesy, there is nothing to prevent leasing brokers or landlords from holding more than one deposit simultaneously on the same space. Therefore, there is no advantage to the tenant who makes a deposit, only an advantage to the leasing broker who is holding your deposit.

2. Demonstrate That You Are Not a Security Risk

Most tenants do end up making a deposit on their lease. Surveys done at my seminars show that only 20 percent of tenants successfully negotiate for no lease deposit. Often it comes down to your ability to demonstrate that you are not a security risk.

Professionals such as doctors and dentists are generally not considered a security risk, but retailers are more prone to industry trends and seasonal economics, so a retailer or restauranteur would be considered by landlords as higher risk. Once, I met a retailer who had more than 30 stores. He proudly told me that he had never missed or been late on a rent payment. My advice to this tenant was to use that great track record to his advantage when renewing leases and opening new stores. Landlords and brokers like to hear that you pay your rent on time, so tell them.

 Be prepared to toot your own horn. If you started in business 12 years ago with a single office but now operate in 6 major cities with 87 employees, you are a success, not a risk to the landlord.

One of my clients provides a detailed financial statement on his company including a recent Dun & Bradstreet credit check on his business to landlords he wants to lease from. When you can present this kind of information with the offer to lease, you have a valuable tool with which to negotiate the lease and negate the deposit requirement.

3. When Should You Give a Deposit?

The offer to lease usually states that a deposit will accompany the offer to lease about to be signed. Beware! This is not necessary and never advantageous for the tenant. If you are prepared to actually give the landlord a deposit (in trust with the leasing broker), it is better to state in the offer to lease that the deposit will be paid within 72 hours of landlord acceptance of the offer, or even upon removal of all conditions by both parties. This way, if the offer is not accepted, you are not waiting for a refund. More importantly, though, giving an upfront deposit is damaging to your negotiating position.

Alternatively, if under pressure from the broker you could make out a postdated check so that the deposit is paid on opening day or the commencement date of the lease term. If the deposit is large or you are short on cash, try to negotiate to give one-third of the deposit up front and the balance 24 hours before opening your business in the premises. The key here is to not give a deposit until the deal is signed and done...if at all.

4. Who Should Hold the Deposit in Trust?

There are many stories of tenants having to wait months to get their deposits back. In the 1980s, when I owned several restaurants and before getting into commercial real estate, I made an offer to lease and, not knowing any better, included a deposit. The deal fell through because of use clause restrictions. I then had to phone every week for over a month trying to get my deposit back. Don't let this happen to you.

 It is safest not to rely on a verbal agreement from the leasing broker that your deposit check will be held in trust by the broker. Why take a chance?

Ideally, your deposit should be held in trust by your lawyer. A second option is to place it in trust with the landlord's lawyer. Your last choice should be to let the broker or landlord hold the deposit. A tenant for whom I was consulting wrote a big deposit check to the broker against my advice. The broker had done a number on this tenant telling him that without a deposit the landlord wouldn't deal and that other tenants were looking at the same space and so on. Shortly thereafter the deal fell through and the tenant was forced to sue the broker to get his deposit back. Being right is of little comfort in such situations if you can't get your deposit back.

5. Negotiating the Amount of the Deposit

As mentioned earlier, tenants are often asked to provide the first and last months' minimum rent payment as deposit. This was the case for a doctor client of mine. She was prepared to pay the full $3,453 deposit before I suggested we offer only $1,000 instead. The landlord accepted the reduced deposit of $1,000 without batting an eye. As with my client in Virginia (mentioned above) the difference between a $60,000 deposit and a $14,000 deposit represents a major win for the tenant.

By negotiating the amount of the deposit, rather than whether you will or will not make a deposit, you create a win-win situation. The landlord can collect a deposit, but it can be an amount small enough so as not to be a hardship to you.

6. Applying Deposit to Future Rent

Most lease agreements call, in part, for the deposit to be applied to the last month of the lease term. Many landlords are flexible on this point to the extent that you can negotiate for the deposit to be applied to a particular month of future rent. Whether it is applied to month 12 or even to month 36, it is better for you to have it applied early than for it to be held until month 60 of a five-year term.

Often I negotiate for the deposit to be applied to the month directly following the free rent period, for example, if months 1 through 5 are free, the deposit is applied to month 6. Another approach to consider, especially if the deposit is large, is to apply half of the deposit to certain months — half to month 18 and half to month 36, for example. This still avoids having to wait until your last month at the premises to have it applied.

Do not be misled by leasing brokers who tell you they can't do the deal without a deposit on the last month of the lease. Remember, the landlord did not construct or buy this building to collect deposits but rather to collect rents. More often than not, deposits are quite negotiable.

Never agree to have your deposit held for the whole lease term, supposedly to be refunded when you move out. If the building you are in is sold or goes into receivership, you may have trouble getting your money back. Beware that some landlords will also attempt to deduct from the deposit wear-and-tear costs attributable to the tenancy.

7. Taking the Deposit Off the Tenant Allowance

If startup money is tight you may be able to negotiate for the landlord to take the deposit off your tenant allowance. This is a particularly good tactic if you are starting up a new business or relocating, and are short of cash.

Try to negotiate this point after you have negotiated the tenant allowance. Even if the landlord accepts half of the deposit in cash up front, with the balance being deducted from the tenant allowance, your start-up or cash flow situation will be improved.

This practice of deducting the deposit from the allowance is reasonable to many landlords, so don't hesitate to bring it into your negotiations.

8. Waiving the Deposit for Lease Renewals

After signing a lease renewal agreement, many tenants receive a letter from their property manager asking for the original deposit to be reinstated. If your deposit on the original lease was to be applied to the last month of the term, you will no doubt be caught off guard by this letter.

Most lease renewal agreements state that except for changes or amendments included in the renewal agreement, the landlord and tenant agree to abide by the original lease agreement for another term of x number of years. In all likelihood, the original deposit clause says that the tenant will continually maintain the specified deposit while occupying the premises. If you have completed your first lease term and are renewing your lease agreement, you are probably not considered a security risk. You do not want to become one of those tenants who are leasing space into their second or third term and still have a deposit down on their lease.

When signing a first-time offer to lease that includes a deposit, simply add (in writing) that no further deposits will be required for additional renewal or extension terms. If you are negotiating a lease renewal, you should include a provision that states that no further deposits will be required for this renewal term, future renewal terms or any extension terms.

9. Transferring Your Deposit When You Sell Your Business

What happens to your deposit when you sell your business? There are several possibilities.

First, you could have the buyer of your business pay a deposit to the landlord and then have the landlord return your deposit to you. However, this is often time-consuming. You are better off including a clause in your lease agreement that allows for your existing deposit to be transferred to the buyer of your business in conjunction with the lease assignment agreement. You can then have the buyer pay you the deposit money up front when the deal closes.

If you are planning to sell your business but did not include this deposit transfer clause, your landlord may agree to it anyway. You won't know unless you ask.

10. Using a Letter of Credit in Lieu of a Cash Deposit

A letter of credit is like a demand note signed by your bank to the landlord for a certain amount of money. Usually you pledge some collateral, such as your house or car, against the letter of credit. If you default on your lease agreement, the landlord can get the deposit money from your bank. A letter of credit will normally cost you between $300 and $500 each year.

For tenants in a good financial situation with low risk of defaulting on their lease agreement, a letter of credit can be a convenient way to make a deposit without tying up all your working capital. Beware of the risk though!

You should also consider reducing the amount of the deposit or letter of credit each year. In some cases you will need to renew the letter of credit every year anyway. It could be for $25,000 the first year, $15,000 the second year, $5,000 the third year, and none thereafter.

The problem with a letter of credit is that it's too easy for the landlord to cash in at your bank. Even if you only miss one rent payment they cash in the letter of credit for the full amount.

When it comes to negotiating your lease deposit don't hesitate to be creative. Very few lease deals fall through simply because of a deposit.

CHAPTER 11

NEGOTIATING A RENT REDUCTION

Several years ago, the owner of a dry cleaning shop came to me. He was nearly broke and could afford to pay only about half his rent. After analyzing his situation, I told the tenant to write a check for half the rent. I then instructed him to go to the property manager's office and put the check for the partial rent payment and the keys to his store on the property manager's desk. It took guts, but the tenant did it. The property manager picked up the partial rent check and gave the tenant back his keys so he could stay in business.

There are two main ways to get a rent reduction: rent abatement and temporary rent relief. A rent abatement generally forgives rental arrears or reduces the monthly rent payment for a period of time with no expectation that the tenant will pay it back. Temporary rent relief is relief for an agreed upon period, for example, six months, in which the landlord agrees to accept less than the regular rent, but may expect to be paid back at a later date. Although you may find it easier to ask the landlord for rent relief rather than a rent abatement both situations are more common than you might realize. Be even more creative if necessary, all they can do is say no.

1. Justify Your Need for a Rent Reduction

Landlords are more likely to grant a rent reduction if you can justify your need for one. For example, when the government reduced health care spending in my area, it adversely effected physiotherapists — a story that was well covered by the media. Every physiotherapist who had hired me for lease negotiations, even those with personal guarantees on their leases, had, within months, received a substantial rent reduction due in part to their circumstances but also in part to the way I presented and negotiated their situations with the landlords.

If asking for a rent reduction, present your case to the landlord using back-up material to justify your need for a rent reduction.

Don't hesitate to open your books and show the landlord financial statements — he or she will usually request this type of evidence anyway. A small pet store owner was experiencing low sales, resulting in insufficient cash flow to pay her rent. By looking at the daily sales records for the past six months, we could see the exact week that sales at her pet store began to decline. It was also the same week that a large national pet store chain (eight times the size of her store) opened up only a few blocks away. The tenant's sales plummeted and stayed low as a result of this formidable competitor entering the market, and her accounting records proved it to her landlord.

Retailers can experience drastic downturns in sales if the tenant mix in their strip mall or shopping center changes. When a major grocery store closed out of a shopping center, the dry cleaner next door suffered lost sales because of reduced traffic. When the landlord then leased the grocery store space to a sporting goods shop, there was little hope the dry cleaner would ever recover to its previous sales level. The dry cleaner was justified in asking for a rent reduction.

2. Ask for More Than You Need

As you may have noticed, asking for more than you really need is a key strategy when negotiating a lease. This strategy is, of course, useful when negotiating a rent reduction too.

A day-care owner once came to me for help. She could not afford to pay her rent of $3,500 per month, and her lease was coming up for renewal. I asked how much of a rent reduction she needed to keep her business viable. She responded by saying that a $500-per-month reduction in rent would be adequate.

 Remember that landlords expect you to negotiate, so don't disappoint them, and ask for more than you need!

I did my homework and then approached the landlord on the tenant's behalf, opening negotiations by insisting on a $1,000-per-month reduction. After a few months of negotiations, we settled on a rent reduction of $800 per month for the upcoming five-year renewal period. As well, this reduction was negotiated to be retroactive to when I became involved, about nine months before the actual lease expiration. I also negotiated a non-repayable tenant allowance to upgrade the daycare's playground.

At my seminars, when I tell tenants to ask for more than they need, or to negotiate for more than they want, everyone nods their head in agreement. However, this month I am working with two great clients whom I am coaching through the lease negotiation process. Both tenants, a chiropractor and a graphic designer leasing office space, understand my advice intellectually. Unfortunately, they simply don't have the guts to put this policy into practice. Face it, we all do or neglect to do things we should even though we know better. Reading this book won't help you if you can't, won't, or don't put these tactics and strategies into practice.

3. Take Your Request to a Higher Power

Most property managers are not empowered to grant a rent reduction, so unless you go above their heads, your requests may be falling on deaf ears. There is nothing more frustrating for a tenant than negotiating for a rent reduction for two or three months with the wrong person, only to be passed to another company official.

Either write to or call the person in charge. You may prefer to make an appointment so you can meet with him or her directly. It is imperative that you have a figure or rent reduction amount in mind and a date when you want it to become effective. Ask for a response by a certain date, about seven to ten days after your conversation or the date you wrote the request letter, and be prepared to argue your case.

4. Make Your Rent Reduction Request Frequently

How often should you ask for a much-needed rent reduction? The minimum is once per month. Many landlords will not take your first request seriously. They believe that if you really need a rent reduction, you will ask and keep on asking. You must put your requests in writing. This will help prevent any mix-ups if the property manager is replaced or the building changes ownership, as you will have a paper trail showing your attempts at obtaining a rent reduction.

Each month when you pay your rent is a good time to include a letter stating your need for a rent reduction. You should also consider sending a copy of the letter to other company officials to make sure you are being heard loud and clear. Don't assume your letters make their way up the chain of command on their own — send them to each official yourself by way of separate envelopes. Phone calls, backed up by letters, are also necessary and effective.

5. Offer to Pay Operating Costs Plus a Percentage of Sales

No landlord likes to receive percentage rent in lieu of the actual amount that was to be paid. Nonetheless, to many landlords, some rent or cash flow is better than none. A tenant's offer to pay percentage rent also demonstrates the tenant's sincere desire to pay what they can.

A good offer would be to pay the operating costs plus 6 percent to 10 percent of your gross sales. Don't be surprised if your landlord's first response is no. Keep asking and keep negotiating.

Many landlords will accept such a proposal after prolonged negotiations.

6. Renew Your Lease Early, At a Reduced Rental Rate

Suppose you have 14 months left on your five-year lease term. You are currently paying $17 per square foot, but the market has softened since you first moved in, and new tenants are leasing right beside you for $12 per square foot. Don't wait until your lease expires: negotiate a lease renewal or a whole new lease effective immediately, at the lower rent. After all, the landlord doesn't expect to get more than $12 per square foot from new tenants, so why should you be paying more?

 If the market softens, don't wait until your lease expires: negotiate a new lease or renewal right away.

In exchange for the reduction now, you are giving the landlord another multi-year term. It may even be to your advantage to blend the balance of your current term with a new five-year term. This is done in a way similar to the way home mortgages are blended when interest rates go down.

A group of dentists leasing over 3,000 square feet hired me almost two years before their lease expired. I was able to get them a $7 per square foot rent reduction for a five year renewal term (almost 50 percent lower than they were currently paying). In addition, I successfully negotiated for the rent reduction to kick in retroactively to when the tenant signed the lease renewal agreement, more than a year before their current (higher rent) lease even expired.

7. Taking the Rent Reduction

What if the landlord ignores you or simply says no to a rent reduction or temporary rent relief request? You can either accept this response or be more proactive. Some tenants just take a rent reduction, and begin paying less rent each month. Technically the tenant is still on the hook, but at least the landlord will finally believe that tenant can't afford to pay what he or she has been paying. Be aware that not paying your full rent each month will put you in default of your lease agreement. However, most rent reductions are given to tenants who are already in arrears. As long as you are actually paying your rent, the landlord will likely think that things can't be all that bad or you would already be behind in your rent payments.

If you decide to take matters into your own hands put a letter in with your next rent check stating clearly and concisely why you have had to make a partial rent payment. Be businesslike. Make sure you offer to meet with the landlord to discuss your situation. If there appears to be a rainbow at the end of your situation, tell the landlord about how you expect business to pick up, and so on. A surprising number of landlords or property managers will accept partial rent payments under such circumstances.

CHAPTER 12
OTHER NEGOTIATING POINTS

1. Negotiating Vacancy Protection

If the success of your business depends on traffic flow or tenant mix, you need some form of vacancy protection. For retailers, this is essential. Look around the property, and ask yourself what would happen if any of your neighboring businesses closed out or moved. How would you be affected? Too often, retailers take their neighbors for granted — until they are gone.

I recently received a call from a retailer who was all by herself in a small retail complex. At one time the complex had been full, but because of excessive rents, her neighbors had gradually all moved out. Now she was stuck in the complex by herself with no walk-by traffic. Consider how other tenants around you will affect your business. Safeguard yourself in the offer to lease stage.

If your business relies in whole or in part on traffic flow generated by anchor tenants you may need some form of vacancy protection in case those anchor tenants move.

When a Safeway grocery store in a retail complex closed, and was replaced by a sporting goods store, it changed the traffic patterns dramatically, affecting all other tenants. If you are signing a long-term lease or renewal it pays to confirm that this won't happen to you. In another center, sales for a local bakery dropped permanently by 30 percent when the landlord leased the space next door to an adult video store. Protection from these undesirable circumstances is often negotiable in advance. If the landlord won't give you written assurances that these events will not occur then you must take that as a sign they could occur.

During the offer to lease stage negotiate for a certain reduction in your rent if a particular tenant, especially an anchor tenant, relocates or changes unfavorably. Insert a clause into the lease agreement that states that you, the tenant, will receive a certain percentage, perhaps 25 percent, off your rent if a certain tenancy is not maintained, or if the building is less than 75 percent occupied. You may also wish to include a clause stipulating your right to terminate the lease agreement if the vacancy reaches 50 percent for a three-month period. The point is to not get trapped into a situation where your business suffers.

2. Heating, Ventilation, and Air-Conditioning (HVAC)

Premises in most strip malls and industrial buildings include a heating, ventilation, and air-conditioning (HVAC) system. Each system serves the needs of a particular tenant. The HVAC units will either be on the roof of the building, on ground at the rear of the building or mounted from the ceiling of the premises. Larger spaces often have multiple HVAC systems.

Many lease agreements stipulate that tenants are responsible for the HVAC-unit maintenance, repair, and possibly even replacement. Negotiate this responsibility back to the landlord. Failing this, your offer to lease should state that the landlord agrees to provide a verifying report that a certified technician has inspected and made any necessary repairs to the HVAC unit(s) before you take possession of the space, much like having a mechanic check a used car before you buy it. The older the building, the more important it is to make this stipulation. A typical HVAC system lasts up to 20 years if properly maintained, so if you're leasing space in a 15-year-old building and the HVAC system is dilapidated, it could cost you major repair money.

Tenants are generally also responsible for hot water heater tanks, toilets, and fluorescent light bulbs — if located within the premises. Ask that these be checked by the landlord and put into proper working order as part of your offer to lease if they are coming with the premises that you are planning to lease. Otherwise the lease will state that you are accepting these items as is. The older the property the more meticulous you need to be about these types of deficiencies. For lease renewal tenants you will automatically be accepting these items in as is condition.

Remember, unless otherwise stated, you are leasing the premises as is. Don't assume anything is working properly or at all. Flush toilets, turn on the hot water, open the rear overhead door, fiddle with the thermostat, open and close the sliding grill door, check for carpet that is coming unraveled, or whatever pertains to the space you are considering leasing. Then negotiate to have the landlord make repairs as part of the offer to lease.

3. Signage

Don't forget to negotiate your signage requirements. Most tenants neglect to do this and simply take whatever the landlord offers.

There are two things to ask for in terms of signage: a less expensive monthly fee or a certain amount of free signage. If you can't get the landlord to come down on the monthly sign rental cost then request at least one month of free signage up front for each year of your lease term.

Chances are that blank signage isn't making the landlord any money, so he or she can easily give you some free months if it means closing the deal. Remember to follow the rule of asking for more than you need or expect to get. Open your free signage negotiations by asking for at least the first year free. If you get it, great! If not, you will likely get at least five months free on a five-year term. Not all landlords will give free signage, especially if signage is in great demand by other tenants. Don't assume signage comes with your premises — you must put it into the offer to lease.

Landlords usually expect you to arrange and pay to have existing signage changed to reflect your company name. If you are negotiating for a tenant allowance, try to get the sign change costs included, especially if it just means changing the vinyl cut lettering.

4. Parking

Landlords are often flexible on parking issues. Just as with negotiating for free signage, I recommend you try negotiating a reduced price for parking first. If that fails, ask for at least one month of free parking for each lease year.

Most high-rise office buildings allow each tenancy a certain number of stalls. This is usually based on a formula, such as 1 stall per 950 square feet leased. Therefore, a tenant with a 3,000-square-foot space will automatically be entitled to three parking stalls. The tenant still has to pay for these parking stalls, but the rate may be negotiable.

If you need more stalls than are assigned for your space, negotiate for them now. Don't assume additional stalls will be waiting for you or your employees once you move in. The building my company previously leased space in was at about 90 percent occupancy but all the underground parking was taken. The list of people wanting monthly parking was so long the building manager wouldn't even add any more names to the list. So if parking is important to you, check it out carefully in advance.

Not all parking is created equal. Surface parking, underground parking, rush parking, tandem stalls (one car behind another) — there are many types of parking spaces. Be sure to check out what other local buildings are offering in terms of parking, and use this knowledge to your competitive advantage.

Location of the parking stalls is also worth negotiating. Go on your own or have the leasing broker take you right into the parking garage and view what is available. Consider the stalls' proximity to elevators, etc.

Constantly fine-tune your negotiating skills. Don't just tell the leasing broker that you need 12 parking stalls. His or her response may be that you are only entitled to four stalls and the parkade is full.

Instead, say something like, "It looks like I can lease this space if I can have 12 parking stalls. If you can help solve this problem, let's do the deal." Let the broker get creative.

By going to the adjacent building, the broker might be able to pick up 3 stalls for you. The lot across the street has 5 surface stalls available. By checking the parking roster, the broker learns that another tenant is downsizing and a stall will be available in three months. You now have your 12 stalls and your employees will have a guaranteed place to park!

If you pay for parking in your building by the hour but often work evening or weekends too negotiate free access to the parkade during off hours. This means that if you come to work, let's say on a Saturday morning or Thursday evening, you can park in the parkade without paying, since the parkade is empty anyway.

Some tenants require customer parking. This should also be arranged in advance. If designated stalls are not possible, make sure you confirm the parking validation policy if any. Being able to give your best customer a token to get them out of the parkade for free has an intangible but real value.

In one instance my client, a midsize office tenant had fallen in love with a particular downtown building. However, underground parking was high on the tenant's wish list. Since this particular building had no parking whatsoever — underground or otherwise — I advised the tenant to pass and find another building.

If a building's parking lot is fully leased, you may be able to negotiate for guaranteed parking elsewhere — across the street or in another building connected by a pedestrian walkway. The leasing broker should be able to help out here since he or she surely comes to this impasse every time they show space in the building. You should also insist that you be put on a priority list for upcoming parking spaces in the building's parkade.

5. Moving Allowance

If a leasing broker or landlord has been trying hard to persuade you to move into a certain building, you can often easily negotiate a moving allowance. Itemize each cost for the landlord. For example, if you have seven sales representatives who will all need new business cards as a result of the move, take the time to get a cost quote from your printer. Telephone and fax hook-up, parking you have prepaid in your current building, moving company expenses, and change of address costs at the post office are all expenses that might be incurred with a move, so don't ignore them. They are often recoverable, even if you are simply relocating from one floor of an office tower to another. The more organized your list, the easier it is to negotiate.

I like to bring the relocation costs out for negotiation after most of the major business terms are pretty much agreed to. However, instead of getting the tenant's moving costs back in money, I settle by taking free rent.

If the landlord says no to your proposal, don't give up. Ask that he or she cover half of your expenses. If the leasing broker agrees to pay half your moving costs, don't settle there. Chances are they will be willing to pay 75 percent or even 100 percent of your costs if it means closing the deal.

6. When Selling or Buying a Business

If you are selling your business and assigning the lease agreement, you will want to be released from any further liability once you turn over the keys to the new owner. Since most lease assignments agreements do not release the original tenant from liability, make sure you add this to the offer or formal lease agreement. Stating in the agreement that six or twelve months after assigning the lease, you and your business will be released from further liability gives the landlord some breathing room to make sure the existing tenant is doing okay, paying the rent and fulfilling the their obligations.

If you are buying a business, confirm everything you are being told about the lease agreement for yourself by requesting and reading a copy of the lease agreement. Talk to the property manager to get a feel for whether everything is okay with the selling tenant and whether the tenant has the landlord's blessing to sell the business. Most lease agreements require that selling 50 percent or more of the shares in a company, or assigning the lease agreement, be with landlord approval.

Millions of people buy residential homes each year and rely on an independent home inspection company to check things out. It has become a big business because people are willing to pay for protection and peace of mind. If you believe in home inspections, and plan to buy a business (thereby assuming their commercial lease agreement) let me encourage you to have a certified lease consultant do a thorough point by point lease inspection in advance. It could save you thousands of dollars. In one such case, my client was planning to buy an existing fast food outlet. After doing my lease inspection and speaking with the landlord I discovered that the landlord planned to relocate the entire food court in a few years. Since the tenant would be expected to pay for all relocation costs it was no longer worth actually buying the business. If you are buying a business and want to avoid an unhappy ending to your story, have the lease agreement inspected in advance.

CHAPTER 13
HIRING PROFESSIONALS

1. Hiring a Certified Lease Consultant

During the 1980s and early 1990s I worked for landlords, leasing and managing their properties. However, in 1993, I switched to the other side and began exclusively working for tenants. The response from business owners and tenants was even greater than I had expected. Ever since The Lease Coach® System was conceived, we have steadily grown to the point where soon we will have an office in every major city in North America. Every year, we successfully complete thousands of consulting projects for tenants. The most popular service we provide is negotiating lease renewals for tenants who don't want to be at the mercy of their landlords. A Certified Lease Consultant will level the playing field and make sure you get the best advice and the best deal possible.

There are several important benefits to hiring a professional Certified Lease Consultant.

First, true lease consultants do not work on commission or a contingency. This means that true lease consultants represent your best interest, not the landlord's. Beware of people calling themselves "tenant representatives": they are often brokers in disguise as lease consultants who promise to represent tenants but who actually collect a commission from the landlord. In general, you can trust that what a true Certified Lease Consultant tells you is in your best interest since he or she has no other motivations or masters to serve.

Second, a Certified Lease Consultant will meet in person with leasing brokers, property managers, and landlords to negotiate your position. As a Certified Lease Consultant, I travel both within my city and to other cities for my clients. At The Lease Coach® we do site selection and even inspect the premises for a new tenant. A large part of our business is simply coaching and consulting tenants who need some advice or guidance.

Third, a Certified Lease Consultant's experience reviewing leases, negotiating deals, writing offers to lease, and their familiarity with the commercial real estate industry and its major players is invaluable to any tenant. Some years I review more than 100 leases, helping tenants avoid dangerous clauses and adding those clauses needed to protect them. Many tenants have used lawyers and attorneys in the past to review their documents, but most lawyers are not professional negotiators, nor do they have extensive commercial real estate experience or background. In fact, each year, lawyers hire us to negotiate their deals and work for them. While lawyers will write letters for tenants very few will actually go to the site and look at the property or get face to face with the broker or landlord for negotiations.

For more information on The Lease Coach® services, self-help books, videos, CDs and tapes or upcoming seminars visit <www.TheLeaseCoach.com> or call 1 800 738-9202. We will send you a free information kit including a rate sheet of our services and fees. If you have questions about your lease or wish to communicate with the author send e-mail to <DaleWillerton@ TheLeaseCoach.com>. All inquiries will be answered promptly.

AFTERWORD

Negotiating is both an art and a skill. By following the strategies outlined in this book, you will be better equipped to negotiate a lease agreement that works for you. Good luck!